literary voices #1

Jeffrey M. Elliot

R. Reginald

THE *Borgo Press*

San Bernardino, California

MCMLXXX

For My Mother—
Who Is Always There
with
Encouraging Words of Love and Support

Library of Congress Cataloging in Publication Data:
Main entry under title:

Literary voices.

(The Milford Series: Popular writers of today ; v. 27)
1. American literature—20th century—History and criticism. 2. Authors, American—20th century—Interviews. I. Elliot, Jeffrey M.
PS221.L528   810'.9'0052   80-12768

ISBN: 978-1-4344-3428-9

Produced, designed, and published by R. Reginald and Mary A. Burgess at The Borgo Press, P.O. Box 2845, San Bernardino, CA 92406, USA. Composition by Mary A. Burgess. Cover design by Judy Cloyd Graphic Design. Some paste-up assistance on this book was furnished by Irene Frost.

First Edition———October, 1980

INTRODUCTION

When asked by Jeffrey Elliot if I'd write an introduction to his new book, I felt pleased to share with its readers my accumulated impressions of Jeff the person as well as the interviewer. Also I felt that the illustrations which *Literary Voices* offers of a fine interviewer at work should serve many writing students as excellent teaching examples. And I think that people who enjoy the armchair study of authors will gain further insights into the myriad facets of the craft of writing.

My initial acquaintance with Jeff came as his subject for one of the interviews contained herein. *Being* interviewed intrigued me, because years ago, seeking some writing niche for myself, I'd had the luck to initiate the *Playboy Interviews*, which for years afterward were my principal activity. So with Jeff across a coffee table with his tape recorder I made a private game of trying to guess his next questions, and of now and then deliberately throwing him a curve answer to see how he'd recoup. During that long interview session's experiencing of Jeff's facile mind at work, I came to enjoy both the notably able interviewer and the highly sensitive, humanistic person.

Conducting a good interview is nowhere near as simple as a good practitioner of the art, like Jeff, will make it seem. To do so ideally requires a quick mind, a commitment to truth, a sense of fairness, a natural curiosity, and a personality and manner which subtly encourages the subjects' disclosure of facets of themselves which otherwise they likely wouldn't.

I know of few things more guaranteed to turn off a busy interview subject than an opening query such as, "Well, here we are, now tell me about yourself!" But anyone with whom Jeff has an interview appointment can be certain that he will have researched them in advance—so thoroughly that he queries them with an apparent ease. And here or there, sensing new questions, Jeff picks his spots for them, designed to evoke the subject's seeming volunteering of always further insights into their qualities, philosophies, and whatever other facets may render them unusual among we fellow human beings. Plumbing with any success into these areas can't be planned in advance; it always occurs as an interview is in progress, usually by some unexpected question which triggers the subject's own curiosity about themselves: i.e., yes, what *is* my self-searching answer to that? Yes, what *does* make me tick?

Jeff Elliot's equipment as an interviewer encompasses that he is both a trained scholar and a trained journalist, his academic skills and tools thus complemented by his good reporter's instincts. The results can be seen in this book's interviews. Jeff's advance research is evident within his average questions. It can be seen how, as each session went along, Jeff was both structuring his interview while developing increasing rapport with his subject. In the end, after his necessary editing and tightening, the material is clear, readable, and intriguing. What has required sometimes several long sessions of querying and responding has been neatly distilled into an intriguing half hour or so for readers to enjoy.

Focussing his intelligence, warmth, and sensitivity upon five professional authors for this first *Literary Voices* collection, Jeff Elliot has captured the essence of five very different writing techniques and personalities—from the Jessica Mitford of the hard-hitting exposes, to the Richard Armour famed for trenchant humor, to Christopher Isherwood's poignant recollections, and Robert Anton Wilson's futuristic insights, and my own historically-oriented efforts.

Why do people read interviews? One poll, by a questionnaire, divulged as the predominating reasons: to be entertained and/or enlightened; to find a new personality; to understand better the "real" person behind the public image; and lastly for their potentials of gossip and small-talk. So to judge from what readers say they want, the compleat interview should supply at least some of all these things. But the interview's basic foundation should be an increased understanding, appreciation, and sense of awareness of the interview subject. In this *Literary Voices* case, if Jeff has done his work well, you the reader should feel the want to read afresh, or maybe for your first time, some of the works of the authors whom Jeff interviews.

Jeff's interviews—stimulating, provocative, entertaining—are, in final sum, just plain good reading. I know I've found myself intrigued with four colleague authors' subjective views, not only of themselves but of our profession, as well as of our world and human society in general. It's my guess that through *Literary Voices*, you'll feel you'd also like to be interviewed by Jeff Elliot.

——Alex Haley
Los Angeles, Calif.
August, 1980

Alex Haley and Dr. Jeffrey M. Elliot.

Alex Haley: The Man Behind Roots

"My old cousin Georgia told me something," remarked Alex Haley, "that has galvanized me—and sustained me—ever since: 'Boy, yo' sweet grandma and all of 'em—dey up dere watchin'. So you go and do what you got to do.' " Apparently, Haley took her words to heart. Indeed, his best-selling book, *Roots*, may well be the most important book of its kind ever written. Not only has it captured the attention of millions of Americans, but it has given rise to a groundswell of interest in black history.

It is difficult to describe the impact of *Roots* on the American psyche. Doubleday, its publisher, scheduled a record 200,000-copy first printing, the largest print run for a hardcover book ever published. That inital run sold out in a matter of weeks, and the book has since gone on to sell well over 1,500,000 copies in cloth. The paperback version set records of its own. *Roots* has also been translated into twenty-four languages, and is a best-seller in many countries throughout the world. In recognition of his outstanding contribution to American social and political history, Haley was recently awarded the Pulitzer Prize.

In addition to the millions of Americans who have read the book version of *Roots*, approximately 130 million viewers saw at least some part of the television version—this was the largest single TV audience since *Gone with the Wind* was shown. The Academy of Television Arts and Sciences responded by nominating the television play for thirty-seven Emmy awards, an all-time record. The program was chosen as best "limited" series of the season.

Roots's author, Alex Haley, is a self-taught writer: he developed his talent during a twenty-year career in the U.S. Coast Guard. After retiring from the Guard in 1959, he decided to become a professional writer and journalist. His first book, *The Autobiography of Malcolm X*, won him national recognition as one of America's leading writers. Haley has long been known as one of the best interviewers in the business. Indeed, his question-and-answer session with Miles Davis was published as the first "Playboy Interview." He conducted numerous other interviews for *Playboy*, including feature pieces on George Lincoln Rockwell, Johnny Carson, Martin Luther King Jr., and Henry Kissinger.

Several years ago, I wrote to Haley in San Francisco requesting an interview. *Roots* had only been out for a few weeks, and, like thousands of other letters, my request went unanswered. I wrote again, employing a slightly different approach, but this letter also failed to elicit a response [Haley, as is now well known, was besieged by sackfuls of mail during this period]. I read that Haley had moved to Southern California and had set up an office in Century City, not far from my permanent residence. So I wrote again, this time suggesting another angle for the interview. Still, I received no response. As a result, I pretty much gave up hope of ever reaching the author.

One day while talking to a friend, I learned quite by accident that Haley had rented the house across the street from mine! I worked up my courage and wrote him one more time, this time sending the letter to his new home. The next day I had an unexpected visitor, none other than Haley himself, who informed me that he had never seen my previous letters and that he would be pleased to grant me an interview. Thus began an association that went from stranger to interviewee to friend. But the story does not end there.

After Haley reviewed his schedule, he invited me to his home later that week to do the interview. As is always the case, I brought a tape recorder to the session. And I was glad that I had. Haley was superb—contemplative, gregarious, provocative, illuminating. I hurried home to listen to the tape. The first cassette was perfectly clear. The second tape was . . . the second tape was ruined. Somehow—and to this day I do not know how—the recorder had malfunctioned this one time. It was garbled beyond comprehension.

I felt miserable—and I was at a loss what to say to Haley. I decided to write, telling him what had happened, and delivered the note to his home later that day. After apologizing profusely, I asked for a new interview, but had little hope, knowing the heavy demands on his time.

That evening, knowing that I would be abysmal company, I went alone to a Kenny Rogers concert. All I could think about was Haley and that damn recorder. Midway through the concert, I left. When I arrived home, there was a message waiting: Haley wanted me to call him the next morning at eight o'-clock. I dialed his number filled with anxiety, but he proved warm, kind, and understanding. True or not, he told me that something similar had happened to him when he had been an interviewer for *Playboy*. As busy as he was, his concern was for *me*.

Haley and I did meet again, several more times, and have continued to meet over the years. One could say many things about Alex Haley, about his eclectic talents as a writer, journalist, interviewer, filmmaker, etc. But these are all abstract things, just so many words. More important than his list of career achievements, at least from my perspective, is what he is as a man. Like *Roots*, Haley is a striking testimonial to the dignity and nobility of the human spirit. He is us at our best and the best within us. I love Alex Haley—not just Alex Haley the writer, but Alex Haley the man—that wonderful man who came across the street and said, "What can I do to help? Let's get started!"

*   *   *   *   *

JE: Let's begin by talking about the genesis of *Roots*. Can you recall the moment when the idea, the concept, the dream came alive in your mind?

AH: It never came together in a composite way, as I gather you mean. It came in wisps, in nuances, in unrelated happenings. From the time I first began, when I discovered the material in the National Archives, to the time I actually decided to write the book, probably a year elapsed. Considerably more time went by as I conceptualized the book in my mind, but again, only in vague form. I had no idea what direction the book would take as I began my research. At the outset, I thought of the book simply in terms of doing a family history. I had no thoughts of going to Africa to trace my roots. I thought I would merely write a book about my family in this country, which I knew like the back of my hand. But as time went on, I got the idea of going to Africa. Even with the family lineage slant, there wasn't enough material to put together a book. And I wasn't sure whether I should try to write an abstract history of the black family or something more personal. Finally, after thrashing it around in my head, and scribbling down some thoughts on paper, I decided that the best way to tell about a people is through an individual, or a family, with whom a reader could identify in personal terms. Eventually, it boiled down to focusing the book around the life of Kunta Kinte—his people, his community, his village, and his

6

culture.

JE: Why did your family history fascinate you so, particularly to the extent of investing so many years in trying to understand it?

AH: My family was always deeply interested in its own history. From my earliest recollections, I can remember sitting on the back porch and listening to my grandmother and others reminisce about the family history. They loved to regale each other with the various stories they knew. The stories themselves were new only to me. I can recall those back porch discussions quite vividly. My grandmother, who lived in Henning, Tennessee, would invite all of the family to her home, where they would sit around and discuss the family history. I listened to everything very intently. I didn't realize it at the time, but my family coalesced around its history. As I think about it, my family has always been proud of knowing who they were, and they loved to talk about it. It was kind of natural, therefore, that I would pick it up later as I grew up and became a writer. Actually, I didn't think about writing a book dealing with my family until I began digging into ancestral records at the National Archives that tended to corroborate what they had talked about on my grandmother's back porch in Henning.

JE: Did you ever envision that *Roots* would have such an enormous impact on the American psyche?

AH: At the time I wrote *Roots*, I didn't think it would have an enormous impact on anything. Of course, I had a great hope for the book, but the extent of my dreams were quite limited. I didn't go around doing a lot of dreaming. I was more obsessed with finishing the book. In fact, I probably never spent more than a total of six hours projecting its results. I had great faith in the book, obviously, since I had twelve years invested in it, but I never dreamed it would create the sensation it has in terms of the public response. It is said by some people that *Roots* is the most important book in terms of social change since *Uncle Tom's Cabin*. If that is true, I can only be humbled by that fact. That's all you can be. You would have to be the worst kind of fool to go around thinking, "I'm going to write a book that will change the world." The most one can do, I think, sensibly, is to write the best book that one is capable of writing. You never quite know what it's going to do. Writing a book is very much like having a baby. Once it's published, it takes off and becomes its own entity. That's happening now with *Roots*. Not a week passes but that I don't get letters, or my agents get letters, from people all over the world, who propose some business proposition involving *Roots*—either the book or something derivative of the book—that I've never heard of before. There's really no way to know what's going to happen. You just have to sit back and wait.

JE: Did you ever imagine that it would take you twelve years to complete the book?

AH: No, never. I doubt I would have given it a second thought had I known that beforehand. I couldn't have afforded to invest twelve years in a project of that type. The only reason I did was because I got hooked. I had a tremendous investment in the project, not so much in monetary terms, because I didn't have much money to invest, but my emotional investment was such that I couldn't let go. And believe me, I must have tried to give up the project at least twenty times. But I just couldn't do it. I always found myself easing right back into it again. I would take a job to write an article or something, and it was like a canker in my stomach, just thinking about something else.

JE: At one point, I understand, the prospects of finishing the book seemed so dim that you actually contemplated suicide. Is that true?

AH: Yes. I almost *did* commit suicide. I was writing the section dealing with

Kunta on the slave ship. I had become Kunta in the process of writing the book. Indeed, a writer needs to become his characters if he's going to portray them with feeling and authenticity. I started having ominous feelings when I was in San Francisco. I was at the point in the story where Kunta had been captured. I had written about thirty to forty pages at least three different times. It just didn't feel right. I was very upset and walking around like a zombie. Finally, it dawned on me what the trouble was. How blasphemous it was for me to be sitting in a high-rise apartment with carpet on the floor, overlooking the San Francisco Bay, writing about Kunta Kinte in the hold of a slave ship. So I called my agent and got the money together to make one last trip to Africa. By this time, I remember, people were very impatient with me—my agent, my publisher, my editor—because I had spent all these years on the book, always telling them, "It will be a great book. It will work out fine. It will be a smash," but they had heard it at least fifty times, and they were sick of hearing it. By this time, I had spent maybe nine or ten years. People were sometimes beyond impatient, just this side of rude to me—even those close to me. When I announced I was going to Africa again, it was met on all sides with disgust. But I went anyway. I had learned that vital thing: let nobody, your mother, your grandmother, your agent, your publisher, your producer, let nobody tell you the creator what you should do. The fact is, publishers don't write books. And producers don't write books. And agents don't write books. They're all derivative, bless their hearts. They make their living off of what the author produces. One of the big things that was made of *Roots* was that the author worked twelve long years to bring off this masterpiece. Well, when the poor bastard was working those twelve years, they were calling him all sorts of names. Anyway, I flew to Africa and put the word out that I wanted to get a ship, a freighter, sailing anywhere from black Africa to the United States. I boarded a freighter called the *African Star* from Monrovia, Liberia to Florida. Each night after dinner I would go down into the hold. I located a big, broad piece of timber in there. I took off my clothes to my underwear, and I would lie on this timber through the night, terribly uncomfortable, extremely cold, trying to imagine I was Kunta. Occasionally, I would lapse off into sleep and wake up cold and still. I would go back into my stateroom, almost numb, take a hot shower, and then write hastily on a pad what was on my mind. I kept doing this until the fourth night, when I just didn't want to go back into that hold. I went out on the stern of the ship after dinner and stood there with my hands on the top rail and one foot on the bottom rail, at which point all of my troubles seemed to roll in on me. I was terribly broke, had less than $300 counting everything, and owed virtually everybody I knew collectively about $100,000. It hit me that there was no way I would ever get out of debt. Then I began to think of how much longer it would take me to finish the book. I had lied to the publisher, had told him at least a dozen times I would complete the book in six months. I had at least two years of writing to go and I knew he wasn't going to give me another penny. And then, most of all, it seemed that even with what I was doing, it was still blasphemous by comparison with what Kunta Kinte had endured. Here I was, a paid passenger on a modern steel freighter, and what I was doing was voluntary. I wasn't in chains. Nobody was beating me. I could come up and take a hot shower. Then a thought came to me. There was a cure for everything. All I had to do was step through that rail and drop into the sea. Nobody would miss me, at least not until morning. I would be a splash in time, and it would all be over. I wouldn't owe anybody. The hell with the book. No more of the publisher to contend with. I felt a kind of warm glow, almost a euphoria. I suppose I was within a millimeter of stepping through that rail.

Then I had this eerie experience. I began to hear voices. It was very simple in its way. There was no band playing. There was no loud shouting. I simply heard these voices speaking to me. And in some uncanny way, I knew exactly who they were. They were speaking to me in a conversational tone, saying, "No, you can't do that. You must finish the book. You mustn't quit." And I knew they were Kunta Kinte, and Chicken George, and Tom the Blacksmith, and my grandmother. They were the whole lineage talking to me. I recall wrenching myself loose from that rail and thrusting myself forcibly backwards to get away from the side. I whirled around and fell on my hands and knees near the hatch of the ship. The attraction to go over the rail was still very strong, but I wanted to stay away from the rail and fall toward the hatch, the center of the ship. I finally got myself into my stateroom. I suppose I cried for two or three hours. Everything in me cried out. I went back into the hold around midnight that night, found my timber, and once again tried to become Kunta Kinte. It was that night, for the first time, that I had some kind of feeling that they all approved—that although I couldn't really be in the situation that Kunta Kinte had faced, they understood that I was doing the best I could. And that is how the rest of the voyage passed.

JE: Numerous reviewers have hailed *Roots* as one of the most significant books of our time. What makes it such an important work?

AH: I've heard numerous erudite explanations of the *Roots* phenomenon, several of which are probably correct in one way or another. In my own mind, however, I tend to go back to something my grandmother said many years ago— that is, "The Lord might not come when you expect him to, but he will always be on time." That's the best answer I know how to give you.

JE: Is there something about the book, or, perhaps, its subject matter, which helps to explain the tremendous public response to *Roots*.

AH: Yes. Looking back over the project, I tried to orchestrate the story prior to actually writing the book. Indeed, the book was significantly enhanced by the fact that I devoted considerable attention to the architecture of the story long before I started writing. My aim was to try to strike a responsive chord in the reader. I started with a little boy, Kunta Kinte, and focused on him from the time he was born. The reader literally shares his birth. He grows up and, like all little boys, is universal. You can't help but like a little boy romping around playfully, enjoying life, experiencing its wonders. We watch him, we love him, we pull for him. As he grows up, I try to weave the story around him and his orbit. I attempt to relate what I had learned about the African culture which had spawned him. And so, we become beguiled by him as we share his journey through life. When I say "we," I mean I was as beguiled as anyone else in recounting the story of his life. There were many times when I would catch myself at the typewriter or with pen in hand, feeling as though I were standing off somewhere at the edge of the village watching Kunta doing the things I was writing about at the time. I was totally caught up in his youthful adventures. In another sense, it was a very personal experience. I so enjoyed my own childhood in Henning that sometimes I wish I had never grown up. I had a ball. And so, in a way, I was Kunta Kinte, reliving my own childhood through his boyhood experiences. As Kunta continues to mature, we watch him grow into teenage, a nice youngster still. He is disciplined, respectful, hard working. You can't help but like that kind of youngster. He has his dreams, his hopes, his aspirations. And then he goes off to manhood training, coping with the problems that it entails. By the time Kunta returns home, only to be captured, slavery has ceased to be impersonal. Indeed, it became highly personal to millions of readers who identified with him in human terms, very much as I did.

As a brief aside, I would admit that in a structural sense, that portion of the book dealing with Africa is too long in terms of balance. One of the contributing reasons, however, is that when it came time for Kunta to be captured, I just hated to see it happen. So I took him off on another trip with his little brother, Lamin, to keep that from happening for a while. When he finally was captured, I felt as though I had been hit in the head with a two-by-four. In fact, I was so broken up over his capture, that I quit writing for several weeks. I just didn't want to go back to the book. Before I could actually begin the next section, I had to go off and get my head together.

JE: As you assess the public response to *Roots*, what do you see as its greatest impact?

AH: If I had to boil it down to a sentence or two, it would be that on a worldwide basis, and I say that because *Roots* has been translated into twenty-four languages, that the "Tarzan" and "Jungle Jim" images, as pervasive world symbols of Africa and African people, will be replaced by Kunta Kinte and his brave people. That's the biggest thing *Roots* could ever do. The pernicious effect of these stereotypes transcends all the adjectives I know. Beyond that, I hope it will give a new sense of pride to black people. Moreover, I hope it will help to foster a renewed feeling of appreciation and respect for black people to take greater pride in the slaves, and Uncle Tom, and Aunt Hager, because they did the most important thing in the world—they survived. If they hadn't done that, then we, who descend from them, wouldn't be doing all the fancy things we're doing today.

JE: To what extent can *Roots* be viewed not only as the saga of your own search for identity, but in a broader sense, as man's search for identity?

AH: I think there's a lot of that in the book and in the public response to it. Obviously, the book and the film, but especially the book, touched something deep in all people. It cut across all lines—age lines, color lines, nationalistic lines, ethnic lines, etc. It literally touched something of a DNA-nature. And so, I think your question probably answers itself. In essence, *Roots* touched man's universal quest for identity. Let me give you an example. Not long ago, I was in Paris for a speech. Something happened there which really astonished me. One day some people were taping an outdoor interview with me. I was walking alongside the host, who was talking to me at the same time. All of a sudden, there was this enormous cry, "Alex Haley!" And as it turned out, there was literally a busload of white people, Americans, who piled out of the bus and came running over to where we were standing. The interview stopped in the midst of the confusion. It turned out that these were people from Kentucky who had not known each other a year before, but who had, spurred on by *Roots*, begun researching their family backgrounds in Kentucky and discovered themselves to have French ancestry. Indeed, it was in the genealogical reference places that they had met each other and uncovered their French backgrounds. They had come to France, as a group of sixty-five people, to dig up their records in remote villages and towns. And I happened to walk by as they piled out of their bus. You want to know how that makes you feel?

JE: Has your own quest for identity made you more proud of being black?

AH: No. I'm not sure I would say that. As I indicated before, I come from a family that has a long history of being proud of who they were, and that includes, of course, being black. I can never recall a time when I was ashamed of being black. We were always taught to be proud of who we were. The search for *Roots* did, however, increase my sense of responsibility in being black, particularly now, in that I'm often held up as a role model, or a voice, or a person who is a contributor to the shaping of culture.

JE: What lessons would you hope black people might learn from your own search for identity? What about white people?

AH: Insofar as black people are concerned, and, to an extent, white people as well, the biggest single lesson is that we black people do indeed have an identity, a rich, prideful heritage. We must make a concerted effort to cast off the negative images that have been applied to us throughout history, and which have, in various ways, come to represent an almost self-fulfilling prophecy. If you tell a people that they have no history, that they have nothing of which to be proud, that they are innately inferior, then they will eventually come to believe it. It's that kind of legacy that we must cast off.

JE: Much of your time these days is spent in promoting *Roots*. Has the massive publicity generated by the book significantly affected your private life?

AH: In some ways, it exploded what had been my previous private life. After the initial publication of *Roots*, when there were strong signs that it was going to be an unusual book, various public relations and media people would say to me, "You're going to lose your privacy." And I would say to myself, "That's what you think. It will never happen." At the time, their warning was abstract. I didn't quite know what they meant. I do now, though. Somehow, you don't seem to appreciate your privacy until you lose it. And then, of course, it's too late. The process itself is a subtle one. Suddenly, you don't have time to do things you did previously as a matter of course. In a metaphorical sense, nothing really affects the twenty-four-hour day. It's fixed in time and space. Meanwhile, the demands, the requests, the mandatories that are part of your new-found success seem to grow geometrically in comparison to what they were previously. For example, there was one period when in three days, I gave thirty-three interviews—television, magazine, radio, newspaper. I scarcely ate or slept, and the demands of the press grew almost beyond physical endurance. Moreover, it was often the case that when you were tired, really tired, someone in the press would come in and zing you. I'm not complaining about the press. It's simply a matter of fact. After all, each of these reporters is looking for something which will make his story a little bit different. I can recall one incident quite vividly. One morning I awoke, having had only two hours sleep the night before, after what seemed like dozens of interviews. Some reporter in a group asked me to comment on a criticism of *Roots* that was raised at the time. I said something like, "Very few books which have received the praise that *Roots* has, are not without their critics, including Homer or even the *Bible*." That afternoon I was astonished to see a story on the AP wire which read, "Alex Haley, turning the opposite of humble, today compared his book, *Roots*, to Homer and the *Bible*." That wasn't what I meant at all, and the reporter knew it wasn't what I said. But the point is, he was able to get an unusual slant to his story, even if it was at my expense. There's much more I could say on this point. However, I feel uncomfortable explaining about the pressures of success. After all, I'm never very far from the fact that previous to all this, I had worked for over twenty years praying to God that one day, just a piece of what has happened to me would come true. It was that fantasy which sustained me all those years at the typewriter, pecking away day after day, just hoping for the right break. When a thing like that finally happens, it catches you off guard. I can remember giving seventy-three speeches in sixty days in forty-two states. It was like being in a maze. I can recall during that period of making a point of trying to establish in my mind where I was, lest I slip and mention the wrong city. Overall, it's a test, a challenge, something you learn to cope with the best you can. One of the things that most distressed me was my inability to answer the mail, something I had always prided myself on before. After *Roots* was published,

I was on the road for the next ten months. I was almost never home. In fact, in those first seven months, I was home something like 22 nights. I spent the rest of the time in various hotels around the country. As the public response to *Roots* began to mount, the correspondence came in canvas sacks. It piled up and up and up. I suppose I probably have 25,000 pieces of unanswered mail. I was simply, physically, unable to do anything about it. It was easy enough to hire secretaries to get the mail out, but I had to read it, at least I thought I did. I would feel awfully uncaring if I simply hired someone to answer it all, particularly after people were nice enough to write and tell me how much they enjoyed the book. Perhaps that would be better than not answering the letters at all, but I still try to answer as much of it as I possibly can. For example, this morning I dictated correspondence until around 3:30 a.m. And I plan to dictate for several more hours this afternoon. When all of this happened, I fantasized that I could become identical triplets—one of me would be chained to the typewriter and fed at periodic intervals; another would devote full time to answering the correspondence, telephone calls, personal requests, etc.; and the third would make all of the public appearances, which is a full-time job in itself. Right now, on my desk as of last week, there were approximately 800 speaking requests, all of which are slated for the next six months. That will give you some idea of what it's like. And yet, that's only part of it. I wouldn't even call it the negative side, but rather a facet of the situation. There are also the beautiful things that have happened. Perhaps the most beautiful of all are the many times people pass me, wave to me, recognize me, and cry out, "Thank you." That just warms me to the bottom of my feet. The emotional, positive responses of people—black, white, yellow, brown—are an incredible thing to behold. In fact, one of the greatest wonders to me is how *Roots* has literally transcended all ethnic groups. The identification of Chicano people, of Oriental people, of Indian people, is something I never would have anticipated. They have the feeling that somehow *Roots* is a good thing for them, too. White people of various ethnic extractions have responded extremely well to the book. It shows itself in many ways too numerous to go into now. However, it's all I can do to keep from crying. People don't know it, but I'm often that way. For instance, when I go into a room where I'm scheduled to speak, it's not uncommon for everyone to stand up when I enter. You don't know what that does to me. I have to force myself to keep from crying. It's something that almost overwhelms you when it happens. As a result, I go around pretty emotional these days.

JE: Not only has *Roots* brought you fame and fortune, but it has also cast you in the role of a major black leader. Do you relish that position?

AH: Well, I would quibble with the word "leader." I just don't feel like a leader. I have become a prominent black voice on account of the tremendous media exposure I've received. But I don't have organized followers or anything of that nature, and that's about the last thing I'm seeking. In any event, I will accept the term "voice"; the "leader," I don't feel. I suppose I could have some influence in one direction or another if I went out and spoke for some cause or some candidate. But I don't choose to exercise that role as such. Each person has a role to play. And mine is, I hope, to write books. That's my number one priority.

JE: Has the success of *Roots* helped or hurt your ability as a writer—that is, has it typecast you or given you greater artistic freedom?

AH: I certainly don't think it has typecast me. If I felt I could only write another *Roots* or *Roots*-related book, then I would have typecast myself. In truth, that's the last thing I think. I'm extremely excited over books down the line which, in a sense, have nothing to do with *Roots* or *Roots*-related material. What has happened, however, is that the success of *Roots* has significantly cut into my personal life in so many ways, and to such an extent, that I'm no longer able to write as I once did. Sadly, and I must face it, my life has changed in dramatic ways. It used to be that my main problem was to simply get up enough money so I could afford to get on a ship—which is my favorite place to write—and sail off for two or three months. The problem now isn't raising the money, but getting the two or three months. I would cheerfully, happily, eagerly pay someone, if this sort of thing were possible, $10 an hour to sleep for me, if I could get the benefit of eight hours sleep a night. Unfortunately, it doesn't work that way. As a result, I haven't written a line, a serious line, since *Roots* was published.

JE: Are you concerned about the excessive commercialization of *Roots*, what some people might call the "poster-T-shirt craze?"

AH: Well, I'm certainly not pleased by it. At the outset, I did everything I could to discourage it. My lawyers and I wrote letters to all sorts of people. We soon discovered, however, that it was like standing in a shower trying to protect ourselves from getting wet with our hands. We realized there was no way to stop it. You could spend all your time trying to track down this T-shirt or that poster-maker or whatever. The best I could do was to refrain personally from contributing to the commercialization of *Roots* by refusing to lend my name to any product associated with it. The biggest single thing I did was turn down an offer which would have netted me $250,000 for merely signing my name on a contract in exchange for endorsing a product as the author of *Roots*. Now, once you do that, it's not so difficult to turn down other offers involving lesser amounts. I decided to turn it down because I felt it wasn't compatible with what I took to be the dignity of *Roots*.

JE: Many people wonder whether all this success will spoil Alex Haley, whether it will change who he is, what he believes, and how he acts. What do you think?

AH: One of my blessings is that somehow, in the deepest center of my make-up, I'm never very far from Henning, Tennessee, with its small-town values, going to church, looking after your neighbor, taking an interest in local problems. To tell you the truth, I'm startled by how people respond to me now. I hope I always will be. One incident comes quickly to mind. It makes me quiver even today. Not long ago, I was in a very emotional crowd. A pretty young girl fullbacked her way through the people closest to me and literally fell on her knees, grabbing me with both arms around my legs. I was totally astonished. I remember saying, "What in the world is wrong with you? Get up from there!" And I hugged her because she was weeping. She said to me, "Thank you, you've given us our history. For the first time, I feel proud of who I am." I understood what she was saying. But it would horrify me if I started thinking, "Yes, this is my due." Occasionally, I have an impulse to go out at night and get a cup of coffee, something I would often do in the old days. But every time I do it now, people cluster around me. There's no way to lose myself in a crowd. If I make a call to the head of a studio, I know now that when I say my name, I will be connected with the person. That, too, is a new experience. From where you sit, you can see, just to your right, two cans of sardines and eighteen cents, ornately framed on the wall. It's next to the Pulitzer Prize citation and the Spingarn Medal. Let me tell you why that "picture" is there. In 1960, I was living in a one-room apartment in Greenwich Village, New York. I was literally hanging on by my fingernails, trying to make it as a magazine writer. I was selling just enough to keep going from week to week, sometimes from day to day. Everyone I knew kept telling me, "It's fine to write, but when are you going to get a job?" I kept writing, however, because that's what I wanted to do. One morning a friend of mine called, a man who was with the civil service. He was very excited, and said, "Look, this new job has just opened up. I can see that you get it, but you have to accept it immediately, because it has to be opened to the public at one o'clock." He could guarantee me the job because I had done twenty years in the Coast Guard, which gave me ten extra points and hiring preference. It was Public Information Specialist and paid, I recall, $6,000 a year. Without thinking about it, I said, "No, thanks, I just want to keep writing." It wasn't any great, noble statement. I was just expressing the way I felt. He was indignant because I owed him some money, and he banged the phone down. That afternoon, I was walking around my little room just off Sheridan Square, taking a sort of psychic inventory of my life—where I was and where I was going. Everything I owned was in that little room. A Castro Convertible sofa became my cot at night and an ottoman by day on which my guests could sit if I had any guests. I had my typewriter, paper, books. In my little cupboard, I had those two cans of sardines which were all I had to eat in the world. And I had eighteen cents in my pocket. That's not the same eighteen cents on the wall, by the way. I spent the original eighteen cents on a cabbage for dinner that night. I remember thinking at the time, there's nowhere to go but up. And I put the two cans of sardines in a sack and put it away. Whenever I would move because I didn't have the rent money, I would always take that sack with me. Six or seven years later I sold my first motion picture rights. That's when I had those two cans of sardines and that eighteen cents ornately framed as you see them there today. No matter where I go, it will always be displayed as a reminder of the most important lesson in the world—that when you're pursuing a creative goal, you must hang in there. You must have faith. You must believe.

JE: Has your lifestyle—in a material sense—changed significantly with the success of *Roots*.

AH: If you mean in a monetary sense, then no, it really hasn't. The truth is, I just don't have much interest in ostentation, in the things money can buy. My joys are mostly career-related; for example, digging into a new book. My peak joy is when I am off somewhere, ideally on a ship at sea, in my little stateroom at 3:30 in the morning, writing as well as I can. There's something about being on a ship, that little subtle hiss as the skin of the ship cuts through the sea, that has a magic quality. It becomes almost like hearing your own pulse. It's an extraordinary experience. That's my joy. I read in the newspapers where I'm a millionaire, and I suppose I am, I know I am. But it has been years since *Roots* came out, and I've spent very little buying things. What I did buy, chiefly, was the slickest typewriter IBM makes, because I'm a nut for typewriters and the gadgets that go with them. I also bought some clothes. You see, from the time of my research years, I was seldom out of a corduroy suit. I had two of them, both brown. You didn't have to iron them. Corduroy could be rumpled and baggy, and it was fine. I could get one of them cleaned while I was wearing the other one. Without thinking, I wore those suits to television interviews after *Roots* came out. I seldom saw myself on television because I was there live, not looking at myself, or, if it was a taped show, I would generally be off somewhere else when it ran. But friends of mine would comment to me, "Alex, you just look shabby." What really turned me around, though, was my day at Harvard. I was photographed walking out of a building with a friend. There he was, looking as dapper as anything you ever saw, and there I was, alongside him, looking as rumpled as anything you ever saw. When I came back to Los Angeles, I told my staff I needed some suits. When the word was dropped, with my new-won status as being "wealthy," I didn't even get a chance to go to the men's store. Instead, someone telephoned one of those fancy haberdashers in Beverly Hills, and they arrived one day with a rack of suits. I remember coming in from an interview and there was a line of suits hung up in the living room for my inspection. I looked at the suits, and they were pretty suits, and bought six of them at one time. I never dreamed I would ever do such a thing. I remember, however, that I had to make a decision rather quickly. In the process, I never asked anybody how much they cost. So I really didn't know. I just sort of thought in my head, "Well, they probably cost like suits I bought before, maybe $125 or something like that." So I could afford, I thought, to buy six suits at that price. I just about fell over backwards when I received the bill. The suits had cost $400 to $500 apiece. I gave flat, absolute, direct orders, which I seldom ever do, to the people who worked with me, that I never wanted to hear the name of that store again. I was extremely uncomfortable wearing stuff that cost that much. As for my home, it's rented. I don't want to buy a home until I know when or if I'm going to settle down some place. The real question is whether I'll settle down. I tend to be a nomad. In my family, I'm the "Chicken George."

JE: Finally, I recently read that you donated a great deal of money to establish a special foundation to fund research in the area of African studies. Can you say something about the foundation?

AH: Yes. The Foundation is a reflection of the responsibility I feel as a result of the success of *Roots*. I very much want to do something constructive with the profits from the book. I have no desire whatsoever to own a yacht, or a mansion, or a limousine, or anything else like that. I'm just not interested in those things. Instead, I've established the Alex Haley Roots Foundation. It only bears my name because of the shoe company which has a similar name. Basically, the Foundation is an outgrowth of my desire to put into practice what I believe. I think it's vitally important that black people, particularly those in positions of responsibility, do what they can to help others who aren't quite as fortunate. As a result, I've set into motion this Foundation. It's arranged so I can donate the legal maximum to insure its continued operation. I was fortunate to secure the assistance of my friend, Mr. James Dyer, to head the Foundation. Mr. Dyer, who is a Harvard graduate, worked previously for both the Urban League and the Carnegie Corporation. With the blessings of the Carnegie Corporation, he became Director of the Alex Haley Roots Foundation, which is headquartered in New York, and which began operation in October, 1977. The purposes of the Foundation are still evolving. However, we hope to provide scholarships for post-graduate students who are working in the thematic area which encompasses *Roots*. In addition, we would like to help disseminate course materials at the primary and secondary levels, on a national basis, dealing with solid information concerning black history. Finally, we want to work in connection with Africa, and, in particular, with The Gambia, to help build bridges between black Africans and black people in this country. As you can see, we have an ambitious agenda before us.

Christopher

Isherwood:

Through The

Looking Glass

Although he was born in High Lane, Cheshire, England, in 1904, Christopher Isherwood's name has become synonymous with some of America's best fiction. Few contemporary writers have made a greater impact on the quality and character of American letters. Indeed, Alan Wilde, in *Christopher Isherwood*, observes: "Isherwood's success in finding new forms (or revitalizing old ones) makes him one of the most rewarding and subtle experimental novelists of the last four decades."

Still, Christopher Isherwood has failed to receive the critical attention that would naturally befit a writer of such preeminent standing. It is difficult to explain this lack of literary recognition, although many observers have wrestled with the question. Cyril Connolly, for example, attributes it to Isherwood's "fatal readability"—the view that it is impossible to take seriously anyone who writes so amiably and effortlessly. Some critics, reports Wilde, wrongly associate Isherwood with his chief protagonists, transferring to him those negative emotions they might harbor toward such characters. Others, like Frank Kermode, dismiss Isherwood on the grounds that he "is not serious," employing excessive frivolity as a stylistic and content device.

In her perceptive study of the author, Carolyn Heilbrun sums up the controversy this way: "Since Christopher Isherwood has been denied, or spared, the gifts of widespread fame or fashion, it is appropriate to state that he is the best British novelist of his generation . . . . He is indeed a survivor. His has been a life of extraordinary adventure, accomplishment, and love: he seems to have meant much to many people. It is, in a sense, ironic that he does not have a central place in the literature of our time, but exists peripherally, still spoken of as one of the Auden, Spender, MacNeice group, or remembered only as the creator of Sally Bowles . . . . Muted in tone, self-effacing in manner, his works continue to make a quiet but persistent claim on our attention. One wishes him to be better known, not for his sake, but for ours."

Clearly, Christopher Isherwood is a renaissance talent; his achievements cut across all major literary genres and demonstrate uncommon versatility. An accomplished writer of novels, short stories, and biographies, he also boasts impressive credentials as a translator, playwright, and scriptwriter. Some of his bestknown works include: *All the Conspirators, The Memorial, Lions and Shadows, Prater Violet, Berlin Stories, A Single Man, Kathleen and Frank,* and *Christopher and His Kind.*

Isherwood's life and work are a striking testimonial to his varied interests and multitudinous talents. He has worked as a secretary to Andre Mangeot, the French violinist; has been a private tutor in London; taught English in Berlin; traveled throughout Europe; did script work for Gaumont-British; went to China with W. H. Auden; was a dialogue writer for Metro-Goldwyn-Mayer; worked with the American Friends Service Committee in a hostel for Central European refugees; was a resident student of the Vedanta Society of Southern California; co-edited *Vedanta and the West* (the Society's magazine) with Swami Prabhavananda; traveled extensively in South America; and was professor of English at California State University, Los Angeles, and the University of California, Los Angeles.

In an effort to better understand Isherwood and his work, I visited the author at his hillside home in Santa Monica, California. Like Isherwood, his home is warm, inviting, comfortable; it reflects his love of art, music, and literature. In an elemental way, it harmoniously complements the blue skies, lush greenery, and majestic mountains which dot the outside landscape. It is clear that Isherwood belongs here; that the area agrees with him. Indeed, the casual California life style is reflected in his home—simple, tasteful, beckoning.

During several hours of reflective and often animated conversation, interrupted only by periodic trips to the kitchen to steep a cup of tea, Isherwood was ardent and alert, full of exuberance and pleasantness. He evidenced a sharp mind, a superb recall, and a wry humor. He was secure, contented, at peace; a man who radiated the intelligence, the sensitivity, and the concern which have become the mark of Christopher Isherwood for nearly half a century.

*   *   *   *   *

JE: In a recent work, *Kathleen and Frank*, you chose your parents as the key figures in a love story. What prompted you to focus on their relationship?

CI: I was interested in writing a book about the material which writers use, why one writes about one thing as opposed to another. I was also interested in how different writers deal with similar themes. I did, in fact, present a series of lectures on this topic several years ago at the University of California, Berkeley, entitled "An Autobiography of My Books." In the process of putting together that presentation, I thought to myself, "I don't really know anything about my own family. I've forgotten so much of my childhood." After my mother died, my brother let me see several diaries that she kept throughout her life. I studied them carefully, as well as numerous letters written to her by my father and various other people. The entire project culminated in my book, *Kathleen and Frank*, which explores their relationship. The more I delved into the subject the more fascinated I became with my own family history. I began to see my parents, perhaps for the first time, as products of a certain social class, subject to certain economic forces which dominated England at the time. This insight helped me to view them in a different way, in a more complete way.

JE: What role did your parents play in encouraging you to become a writer?

17

CI: My father played quite an important role. He was an extraordinary man. He was an army officer by profession, but his real enthusiasm was for art and music. He certainly encouraged me in these directions. In addition, he stimulated my interest in the theater. In fact, he encouraged me to put on small productions as a child. I suppose, though, he was a bit amazed by how I turned out. Hopefully, he wasn't too disheartened.

JE: In *Kathleen and Frank*, you act both as the narrator and as a principal character. Does this type of total involvement help or hinder the ability of a writer to convey his message?

CI: It's a difficult technique to use successfully. It wasn't too difficult, though, in *Kathleen and Frank*. The problem loomed larger in *Christopher and His Kind*, which was a more difficult work to write. In that book, I was faced with the naked facts of my own existence, much more so than I was in *Kathleen and Frank*. I did, however, write the book in the third person. I try to make it very clear that it's me, but I call the person "Christopher." It was an extremely interesting book to write.

JE: Did you learn a great deal about yourself in the process of writing these autobiographical works?

CI: No. I don't think I discovered any great revelations, except, perhaps, the thing we must all face—namely, that we can rise to anything because we can also sink to anything. All of us are capable of the most atrocious behavior. We may be prevented from carrying it out, but it is there nonetheless. There's no use in pretending that these motives, these drives, these instincts, are not part of our being. They are! And this is where autobiographical works can prove helpful. If one writes about oneself, the real motive must be, I think, to give reassurance to other people: "Don't worry, the situation is not as bad as all that. I did much the same thing. I survived it. And you will, too." In the end, that's really all one can say to one's fellow human beings. That's what any kind of autobiographical writing should be about. Its purpose should not be to point out one's virtues or, for that matter, one's faults. Rather, it should be to touch a common chord of human understanding. In all my writing, I have attempted to focus on those personal experiences which cut across the gamut of human behavior. I've been extremely pleased, and somewhat surprised, by the response. Usually, after relating something extremely personal, extremely intimate, I will get dozens of letters from people saying, "How did you know? Yes, that's exactly what happened to me last Thursday."

JE: Your youth is skillfully chronicled in another autobiographical work, *Lions and Shadows*. Here you relate the story of a young writer in London in the 1920s. What was the significance of this period in your development?

CI: It was a key period in my life, a period in which I started to establish my own identity. It was a period of profound influences, influences which helped to shape my interests and personality. I emerged from the more generalized world of school and college and began to define my preferences and concerns. I found myself moving in new directions, charged by passionate enthusiasm and excitement. It was a period of great personal energy. It was also a period of great suffering. I experienced pangs of despair, feelings which persisted throughout much of this period.

JE: Throughout your life, you have traveled and lived in many places. You resided in Germany during Hitler's rise to power. Was that a frightening period to be alive?

CI: No, not really. It was much more exciting than frightening. What was really frightening, though, was being a part of a barracks-like world. In this sense, the most sinister experience of my life was being in boarding school.

There, I felt totally at the mercy of other people.

JE: Were you cognizant of the meaning of the events which were transpiring in Germany at the time, what they would lead to, and the consequences for the world community?

CI: No. I was wrong, like most people. I didn't think Hitler would succeed. A lot of great international experts on foreign affairs were wrong, too. They thought Hitler would trip up once he came to power. They never understood that Hitler was serious, that he would stop at nothing. He was prepared to overthrow the constitution which, incidentally, he did quite legally. He succeeded in getting Parliament to vote to overthrow the German Constitution. He was later named Chancellor—again, quite legally, by Hindenburg. He resorted to completely legal steps to take power, primarily, because the underground pressure was so strong. People were fooled. They didn't realize the tremendous force which motivated this man. They thought he would fail to solve the nation's problems. He solved them, though, in his own perverted way; essentially, by putting the nation on a war footing. Looking back, it was certainly not a good period to be a writer. There was a feeling of great dread and uncertainty, a feeling of despair and hopelessness which loomed overhead: "Oh, what's the use? There's going to be a war. Why bother to write this stuff? It will be destroyed anyway." That kind of attitude required a great deal of determination. It was difficult to go on with anything. There was a dangerous mixture of sloth and fear. And there was nothing that could be done about it. I think one must live as though one were going to live forever. One must get on with the business of life. Unfortunately, few people were able to live this way during Hitler's rise to power.

JE: Early in your life, you met W. H. Auden. You went on to have a long and intimate relationship with him, not to mention co-authoring several major works. What were your first impressions of Auden?

CI: I first met Auden when he was about seven years old. I was about ten at the time. We met in school. While we knew each other quite well, we were not particularly intimate. We met again when Auden was in his teens and I was nearly twenty. Then, to my stupefaction, I discovered that he had written a great many poems. I had never thought of Auden as a poet or anything of that sort. Furthermore, his work was extremely good. His poems were quite different from what most prople think of as Auden today. Like many great poets, he started by writing in a style that belonged, quite clearly, to certain other poets. In this regard, he wrote many poems that resembled the style of Hardy and Frost. Gradually, his work took on the most extraordinary kind of power. Even the poems he wrote like Hardy, when he was only about sixteen, were very good. They were at least second-rate Hardy. They were quite striking. Auden had an amazing talent. After I read some of his work, we began to talk with greater regularity. We quickly formed a very intimate bond that survived throughout our lives. Oddly enough, coming to the United States separated us somewhat, not so much in our hearts, but certainly in physical fact. Auden always preferred to live in the East, while I was more comfortable in the West. We saw much less of one another in the latter part of our relationship. Later, of course, he moved to Italy, then to Austria and, finally, to England, where he lived most of his remaining years.

JE: Was Auden a warm man, a giving man, a loving man? Was he easy to get to know?

CI: I wouldn't say he was especially easy to know. He was, however, quite warm. He had a very loving heart. There's no question about that. There was this exterior about him, though, that was somewhat forbidding. He would often scare people off, at least initially. Later, when they got to know him better, they developed a very strong affection for him. Auden was always surrounded by people who loved him. He wasn't, though, what one might call a "social" person, in the sense that he liked to go out and mix a great deal.

JE: What kind of friend was Auden?

CI: The best. He was my best friend, certainly. We shared great intimacy. The truth is, however, I'm not an "intellectual" in the sense that most people define the word. Auden, on the other hand, had a very powerful intellect. He possessed extraordinary learning. He seemed to learn things almost by breathing. He would read books at a speed which would astonish most sight readers. It was irritating when it turned out to be your manuscript he was reading so quickly. I once watched him, in this very house, leafing through something I had written. At the end of the manuscript, he knew everything about it. He had mastered it completely.

JE: What made you feel so close to Auden? What accounts for your deep affection?

CI: Well, first there was that special bond which went back to our child-hood. Although we weren't especially close during that period, we really breathed the same air. Second, we were both homosexuals, but that really applies to many of my friends. It was certainly a great bond, though. Third, I think we both saw things in a peculiarly English way. We had a very similar view of the world. Fourth, we were both intensely interested in literature. In this regard, it helped that we both had different literary interests. From the beginning, Auden was the poet. And that was it. I was the novelist. And that was it. Our literary relationship was very departmentalized, which served to strengthen our ability to work together effectively.

JE: Did Auden play an important role in shaping the direction of your work?

CI: No, at least not consciously. The key people who influenced my work included E. M. Forster, with whom I had what might be described as a "master-disciple" relationship, mainly since he was a good deal older. I loved him very much. Another important influence was D. H. Lawrence, whom I never met, but who was a tremendous inspiration.

JE: Although you're viewed primarily as a novelist, you began your career as a poet. Do you still enjoy poetry and, if so, why haven't you published more poetry since then?

CI: Actually, that whole business about my having written poetry is some-what erroneous. People think I wrote poetry simply because I collaborated with Auden on certain plays which included poetry in them. In truth, I never wrote one word of that poetry. That was always part of the departmentalization of our relationship. He wrote all of the poetry. As for me, I wrote very little poetry and, certainly, no more than all sorts of people who go on to become engineers or surgeons. I certainly didn't write anything of great distinction, with the pos-sible exception of some nonsense verse that have been reprinted several times.

JE: Did you enjoy writing poetry? Did it fulfill a need for self-expression?

CI: Yes. I enjoyed it. I suppose I had a certain facility for poetry. But it never amounted to anything. My poetry never had that special magic. Poetry, unlike writing, never proved to be an emotional outlet for me. It never served that kind of function. It was simply an exercise of ingenuity. Certainly, if I had wanted to say something personal, I never would have resorted to poetry. Instead I would have written about it in my diary. It would have been in prose, though, not verse.

JE: Do you still keep a daily diary?

CI: Well, I keep a daily log, in the sense that I say, "This happened, and I met so and so, and I did such and such." I do keep a personal journal, though, in which I record those things that really interest me. But it's not a daily activity.

JE: In the foreword to your novel, *All the Conspirators*, you state that the book is the work of an "angry" young man. What caused your anger during that period?

CI: When I wrote that book, in 1958, I was in revolt against the establishment, which was personified in the school, in the church, and in my mother and her opinions. My mother and I were very different. We were almost total opposites in terms of our likes and dislikes. We disagreed about virtually everything. However, I've always felt a great deal of affection for my mother, which I tried to point out at the end of *Kathleen and Frank*.

JE: After professing a belief in atheism in the late 1920s, you moved to California, where you discovered Gerald Heard and Aldous Huxley, both of whom were studying Vedanta philosophy. You took an immediate interest in the subject and went on to pursue it at some length. Why did you embrace this particular view of the world?

CI: I suppose it was due to several things. Basically, my specific circumstances at that moment demanded some kind of belief. They demanded a basic kind of reorientation. I had always realized, in a backhanded manner, that I was a pacifist. That feeling probably goes back to the war in China. Suddenly, I had an absolute feeling about the outrageousness of asking any human being to fight for a cause unless he honestly wished to participate in such an effort. I was totally incensed by the idea of conscription. I can certainly understand why two people may want to kill each other. There's no use in pretending that these feelings do not exist. They do! All one can do, I think, is to try to dissuade the two persons from taking this action. But when you create a climate in which one nation is presumed to hate another nation, so much so that it wants to obliterate that nation from existing, then that's something which I find totally incomprehensible. Each of us, I think, must do what we can to bring an end to this madness, which is why I identify myself as a pacifist. I'm opposed to organized murder! I was drawn to Vedanta, though, simply and solely because of the personality of this particular man, this Hindu monk, whom I met through Heard. After watching him, talking to him, being with him, I realized that Vedanta had something powerful to offer me in terms of how I viewed the world. It gave my life new meaning, new direction. It provided a link between life and death. It wasn't so much the philosophy which interested me, but the way in which this monk lived his own life and dealt with various things. He was a totally heroic character. He possessed tremendous inner strength.

JE: Some years ago, you decided to settle in Hollywood, California. You relate your early impressions of life there in two short works, *Los Angeles* and *The Shore*. Do you still enjoy the California life style?

CI: Yes. I very much like living here. I'm really very native to this place, even though I possess so much superficial "English-ness." I've lived here far longer than anywhere else in my life. In my youth, we were constantly on the move, owing to the fact that my father was an army officer. As I grew older, I traveled quite widely. So, really, Southern California is my home, by any definition, except that I wasn't born here. As for the place itself, it has changed a good deal with the passage of years. When I arrived here, it was a rather sleepy little place. It was very sprawling; things seemed so far away. There was an element of romance about the area. Obviously, life here is quite different today. Even so, I'm still quite fond of Southern California.

JE: For the past several years, you've been an outspoken advocate of civil rights and civil liberties, particularly as they relate to gay people. Is this still a pressing personal concern?

CI: Yes, very much so. I'm disgusted by the persecution of homosexuals. It must stop! I don't think you can bulldoze people into liking other people, though. I think some people feel an absolutely natural prejudice against homosexuals, Jews, blacks, and various other minorities. They may not like the sound of their voice, or the way they look, or how they act. They may feel uncomfortable in the presence of these people. Fine! Let that be. Let that serve as a safety valve, if need be. But let us, for God's sake, at least abolish the repressive laws which exist. Let us behave in a civilized manner when it comes to safeguarding other people's rights. We don't have to associate with them, but that doesn't give us the right to deny them the right to live as they choose. We have far too many repressive laws which do violence to innocent people. The time has come to correct this situation.

JE: Some years ago, you publicly announced that you were a homosexual. What caused you to take this action?

CI: I took it for many reasons. Every phase of life brings with it, I think, certain duties, certain responsibilities. Old people, in particular, should take advantage of their respectability, of their veteran status, to make statements of social importance. Each of us must stand up for those things in which we believe. Alas, in my particular minority, there are still a great many people who, for one reason or another, have chosen to live their lives in the closet. It was my hope, in making this statement, that it would put a little gumption into them, encourage them to make similar statements in the context of their own lives. It's a sad thing, but it's amazing how few prominent gay people will admit that fact, will permit themselves to be interviewed by the gay press. It's seen as not nice. It's viewed as disreputable. My friend, Don Bachardy, was interviewed some time ago by the *Advocate*, the nation's largest-circulation gay newspaper. In that interview, he "came out" and discussed our relationship. In fact, there's a picture of us together when we first met. Most people liked the interview, but, alas, some people were terribly shocked. To them, it wasn't socially respectable!

JE: What impact did the announcement have on your career?

CI: It's difficult to assess that sort of thing, particularly in my case, since people have always known about me. I'm a person who has chosen to live most of his life in utter openness. There wasn't anybody who knew me personally, or who knew about me, who didn't know I was a homosexual. If I ever met anybody who didn't know, and who wanted to know, then I told him right off. Actually, I'm a very domestic creature. I've lived most of my life with somebody. It was in *Kathleen and Frank*, though, that I "came out" in the simplest language possible; and that was because it was an integral part of the book. It was absolutely necessary to reveal this aspect of my life.

JE: Several critics have suggested that most of your work, either directly or indirectly, contains substantial autobiographical material. If this is so, why did you choose this intensely personal focus for so much of your work?

CI: Really, what other life experiences does one have other than one's own? I'm very much an existentialist. I only really believe in what I've experienced. I know by inference that what I've experienced, you've probably also experienced. After all, all good writing is essentially autobiographical. Otherwise, it would be extremely difficult to communicate in human terms. Most good writers write about that which they know best, which is their own life. That's nothing unusual. It is true, though, that some writers, such as Ray Bradbury, deal primarily with fantasy and science fiction. But that too is a function of the whole being, just as much as deep-sea fishing was an integral part of Hemingway's being.

JE: In a review of Steinbeck's book, *The Grapes of Wrath*, you make several interesting comments about the relationship between art and propaganda. Is it legitimate to tie art to propaganda?

CI: I think the two are often inseparable. After all, what is propaganda? It is a statement of conviction. Essentially, there are two kinds of propaganda: emotional propaganda and statistical propaganda. One kind stirs emotions in a general sort of way, while the other tries to persuade through cold facts. The latter is more aptly described as "real" propaganda. It's a statement of alleged fact, the product of supposedly impartial analysis. Of course, there's no such thing—certainly not in art or literature. Whatever one writes, I think, contains an element of propaganda. It reflects one side as opposed to the other. It makes certain statements and not others. It espouses certain views rather than others. The point I tried to make in my review, though, was quite different. There, I was concerned with pointing out the dangers of mixing the two kinds of propaganda which, I think, Steinbeck did in that book. In the end, his approach tends to widen the credibility gap. It affords the reader an opportunity to avoid personal responsibility because of the questionable way in which Steinbeck marshals his facts.

JE: When Virginia Woolf died, you wrote an eloquent piece on her life and work. What was she like? Did you have a close relationship?

CI: I really didn't know Virginia too well. I knew her, mainly, because she was my publisher in England. She was like many people who are loosely referred to as manic-depressives. On the one hand, she experienced periods of intense depression, which resulted in several nervous breakdowns. On the other hand, she was wonderful company, as the manic-depressive often is when he's in the manic phase. She was amusing, extremely witty, and a wonderful entertainer. That's really the only part of her I saw. Of course, one could not ignore her beauty. She was one of the most beautiful women I've ever seen, not so much in a conventional way, but in terms of her uniqueness. Her face was incredible!

JE: In your novels, you employ a variety of literary devices, including montage, flashback, and fast-paced dialogue. How important are these techniques to your style of writing? Are you conscious of style as you're writing?

CI: It's very much like working with a set of brushes or a set of tools. One uses them in order to get across one's meaning as effectively as possible. I think, however, I'm getting more and more away from such techniques. I still like my flashbacks, though. They're a basic reflection of my personality. I'm a person who finds it difficult to remain on one subject for too long. It's only natural for me to switch gears to another subject. This produces a somewhat jerky style.

JE: What do you most enjoy about being a writer?

CI: Basically, I like being my own boss. That's very important to me. It's also fascinating work. There's a task to attend to every day.

JE: Are you a meticulous writer? Do you rewrite a great deal?

CI: I edit enormously. I rewrite entire paragraphs, entire chapters, entire books. I often labor over specific words, specific sounds, specific moods. I agonize over every sentence.

JE: Who are your favorite writers? Who do you like to read when time permits?

CI: Well, in addition to Forster and Lawrence, whom I mentioned earlier, I like many of the great Russian writers—Dostoyevsky, Tolstoy, Chekhov.

I also like other writers, such as Kerouac, Pynchon, and Casteneda. Sometimes I like Mailer, especially when he writes about himself. I also like Vidal, particularly his historical works.

JE: Finally, have you ever thought how you might have spent your life had you not decided to be a writer?

CI: Really, writing is my nature. It's an expression of my being. When I'm writing, I'm being me. What else could one be? I don't really know. As one gets older, everything becomes much simpler. One gets a better fix on life, perhaps because death is more present. One learns to adjust to the fact that time is limited. And that's good. I think it makes for a much saner existence. In a way, one becomes more appreciative of the present. Writing affords me the opportunity to be me, to say what I think and express what I feel. So, in the end, I'm a writer because that's what I am. What else could I be?

Jessica Mitford: Pioneer Spirit of Investigative Journalism

Although she was born at Batsford Mansion, Gloucesterchire, England, in 1917, Jessica Lucy Mitford has carved out a reputation as one of America's premier muckraking journalists. Following the historic tradition established by such precursors as Upton Sinclair, Gustavus Myers, and Lincoln Steffens, Ms. Mitford has cultivated and refined the American art of muckraking. Her name has become synonymous with the exposure of fraud, corruption, and injustice. As the *Guardian*'s Lena Jeger has observed: "Her life has been a protest—a protest against her own privileged, aristocratic background; against snobbery and political selfishness and reactionary regimes wherever they exist."

The British-born writer's journalistic approach integrates the techniques of investigation and disclosure, tempered by a penetrating humorous style, which creates an atmosphere of authenticity and credibility. At the heart of her endeavors is Ms. Mitford's overriding concern for the safeguarding of civil liberties and the elimination of human deprivation. The focus of her exposes has run the gamut from the deceptive practices and crass commercialism of the funeral industry to the deleterious consequences of archaic conspiracy statutes; from the underhanded advertising and hard-sell tactics of mail-order writing schools, to the brutal dehumanization inherent in the American correctional system. Her best received works include, among others: *Daughters and Rebels, The American Way of Death, The Trial of Dr. Spock, Kind and Unusual Punishment: The Prison Business,* and *A Fine Old Conflict.*

Ms. Mitford began her journey as an activist-rebel early in life. At nineteen, "Decca" (the name ascribed by her siblings) left home with Esmond Romilly, a nephew of Winston Churchill, to work for the anti-fascist loyalist faction during the Spanish Civil War. The pair, second cousins, were wed in 1937, and emigrated to America two years later. After travelling together quite extensively,

Romilly enlisted in the Royal Canadian Air Force to continue the fight against fascism. When her husband was killed in action in World War II, Ms. Mitford elected to remain in Washington, D.C. to work as an investigator in the Office of Price Administration. She moved to California in 1943, eventually settling in the Oakland area.

During the late 1940s and early 1950s, the author served as the Executive Secretary of the left-wing Civil Rights Congress in Oakland. In 1948, the organization was instrumental in sparking an investigation by the California State Assembly into allegations of police brutality. Ms. Mitford's political philosophy has been a source of consternation on more than one occasion. In 1951, for example, the author was summoned to appear at hearings conducted by the California State Committee on Un-American Activities. She has been denounced in the *Congressional Record* as "pro-communist, anti-American" by right-wing congressman James B. Utt (R-California.) As late as 1970, Ms. Mitford's name appeared on a list, formulated by the House Internal Security Committee (formerly the House Un-American Activities Committee), of "radicals" who had lectured at American colleges and universities. In this regard, Ms. Mitford's well-received autobiography, *A Fine Old Conflict*, skillfully chronicles the author's life, highlighting her experiences as a member of the American Communist Party from 1944 to 1958.

Although she did not begin her professional career as a writer until she was almost forty, Ms. Mitford has made a singular contribution to the field of investigative reporting. Her efforts reflect the transition from the staid tradition of muckraking to the age of advocacy journalism. Whether conducting an exhaustive inquiry into America's "rites of passage," or questioning United States involvement in Indochina, Ms. Mitford strives to raise issues of legal and ethical concern which are both topical and relevant. As a result of her pioneering efforts, she was recently appointed Distinguished Professor of Sociology by San Jose State University, for the purpose of conducting a special seminar on the history of American muckraking.

At this point in her distinguished career, I found the author engaged in a whirlwind promotional tour, touting her new release, *Poison Penmanship: The Gentle Art of Muckraking*. The interview below took place in the teak-wooded living room of her spacious Oakland home, and sprawled over into lunch at a nearby oriental restaurant. In person, Ms. Mitford conveys the same keen-spirited wit, optimistic zeal, and ebullient manner which have become synonymous with her brand of hardhitting reporting; the same qualities which have made her a pioneering voice in American journalism.

*   *   *   *   *

JE: Why did you choose to write your autobiography at this particular point in your life?

JM: Well, I really started it about seventeen years ago, but never could get finished with it. I kept getting sidetracked by other projects, like *The American Way of Death*. Actually, I wrote the first volume of my autobiography in 1960. It was published under the title of *Hons and Rebels* in England, and *Daughters and Rebels* in this country. It was the first book I had ever written. I was about forty at the time, a very old age for a first literary effort. Then I started on a sequel in 1961, but only wrote about thirty pages before I started writing *The American Way of Death* instead. The sequel, which I called *A Fine Old Conflict*, was finally released in 1977. I kept "nosing" back to this whole thing—nosing around the problem of it, and never being able to get very far. Finally, I thought,

"Well, I've got to do it," because I really wanted to, and so then I did it.

JE: Did you find it difficult to write a book which was ostensibly a chronicle of your own life, most notably, your involvement in the Communist Party?

JM: Yes. I suppose that is why it took me such a very long time settling down to do it. I think my whole relationship to the Communist Party was a terribly complex thing to approach. It was very difficult, years later, to get back into that era. When writing about your own experiences, you must somehow absolutely immerse yourself in those days again. One little trick that I find useful, when I have forgotten what has happened, is to read back issues of *Time* magazine in the library. In my view, *Time* is a rotten dirty magazine, the yellowest yellow press. But it will help bring the headlines of the day back to life, and then your recollections come easier.

JE: Was it a painful experience to write the book? Was it hard to deal with the tragedy that surfaced in the course of recounting your life?

JM: Yes. There were many times when the project became quite painful. On the other hand, I skimmed over a lot of those memories. The book itself is really an account of what it meant to be a Communist in those days. I don't think the book comes over as terribly sad. It was a tragic period in American history, but on the other hand, it was an exhilarating time, a point which I hope will come through.

JE: Did it concern you that in writing the book you were laying yourself bare, exposing yourself in the most public way possible? Did you have any gnawing doubts about how much you wanted to reveal about yourself?

JM: No, not really. As I said earlier, the first book I wrote was autobiographical. What I really hoped to accomplish with this book was to bury several myths that had grown up around membership in the Communist Party. I think the book is primarily beamed at people who don't have much background in this area. When you think about it, the House Un-American Activities Committee is ancient history to people who are now entering college. Young students often find it difficult to believe what happened in that period. However, they are keenly interested in finding out about the whole McCarthy era.

JE: How do you know, in writing an autobiography, if you are being fair to yourself and your readers? Is it difficult to be objective about yourself and your motivations?

JM: Yes. Objectivity is a very difficult thing to achieve. In this regard, journalistic ethics and objectivity are not really my strong points as a writer. If objectivity means not having a point of view, then I plead guilty to not being objective. Tracking in everything you know about a subject would be exceedingly boring. I would not attempt such a thing. I have my own point of view about most things, and I want to express it in my writing.

JE: Did you anticipate considerable personal criticism with the publication of the book?

JM: Yes. I was even looking forward to it. I was very disappointed when it did not materialize. What I really expected, above all, was a head-on attack by the Cold War liberals. You see, I rather enjoy being attacked. It gives me a good chance to fight back. You can't fight back if there is no attack. In England, the reviews were mixed. In this country, the book was pretty much taken at face value and received rather good reviews on the whole. Actually, I was quite amazed.

JE: How was your autobiography received by friends and associates who lived through this period with you?

JM: I had no idea how the book would be received. On the whole, most of my friends liked it. That was the best part of having written the book. Mr.

William Schneiderman, who at the time was a formidable leader of the Communist Party, called to tell me the book read like an affectionate memoir of an old friend who somewhere took a wrong turn.

JE: During the course of promoting the book, you had an opportunity to speak to numerous audiences. How did college students receive the book? Were they interested in the McCarthy era and its impact on American society?

JM: Yes, very much so. I did not sense the kind of apathy that many people talk about as existing on college campuses. Perhaps this is because I have done some teaching myself. In 1973, for example, I was invited to teach in the unlikely capacity of "Distinguished Professor" in the Sociology Department at San Jose State College. As you know, after accepting the offer I was fired for refusing to be fingerprinted. I wrote an article about the entire affair, called "My Short and Happy Life As a Distinguished Professor," which was published in *Atlantic Monthly*. The thing that amazed me most was the almost unanimous support for my position from the students and faculty. The student body at San Jose State is extremely diverse in its makeup. I had no idea how they would respond. Actually, they rallied to my side in the most incredible fashion. We went on to win the fingerprint case in court. The news media in this country continue to publish articles, virtually every year, pointing out how apathetic most students are—insisting that today's campuses are reminiscent of the quiet of the 1950s. I discovered that the opposite was true when I taught at Yale University. After my article was published in *Atlantic Monthly*, I received a letter from Yale stating, "We have read your article. We do not require fingerprinting or loyalty oaths. You would be most welcome to teach here." I accepted their offer with great enthusiasm.

JE: Speaking of the country as a whole, do you discern widespread public apathy to the great problems which beset us? Do you think that the disappointment and unrest of the late 1960s and early 1970s served to dissuade many young people from trying to effect meaningful political change?

JM: These are times of great confusion. The trouble today stems from the lack of a consolidated left-wing movement. Eventually, I think, controversial issues will engender greater public interest and help dispel much of the apathy that presently exists. The shootings at Kent State University were sort of the watershed of that entire period. It was a very disconcerting event.

JE: How would you respond to those who contend that the system itself is impregnable and that only incremental changes of an insignificant order can be initiated?

JM: Well, there is much merit in that point of view. The question seems to be: in the end, what good does muckraking do? At best, reforms can only patch up, or gloss over, a few basic flaws in our society. On the other hand, if we don't keep the pressure on, we will have no chance of success. It is vital that we keep our efforts alive. I hope people realize that they're being ripped off by the system. The purpose of muckraking is to see that that doesn't happen. It's that simple!

JE: How do you explain the willingness on the part of many Americans to give away their basic freedoms without even a protest?

JM: In that sense, America is not much different from most countries. For example, look at the laws of England. They are far more restrictive than in America. Most people want to live their lives free from intervention. Their world centers around themselves and their own family. They only get excited about their rights when they personally feel threatened. During the McCarthy period, a well-known newspaper sent a reporter out to conduct a survey on peoples' attitudes toward the Bill of Rights. He presented the document, without identification, to people cornered through chance encounters on the street. The result was a landslide vote against the Bill of Rights.

JE: Have many of the problem areas you've investigated been suggested by average citizens—people who write to you and ask you to look into something for them?

JM: Yes, at times. After *The American Way of Death* was published, I received letters from all kinds of people saying, "This is another thing that needs to be exposed. Won't you help?" I started to file these ideas away by category. I found that I accumulated an enormous number of complaints about defective hearing aids. The hearing aid business, I think, is one of the most rotten rackets that exists today. Personal sound amplification devices are marketed for people who live in misery. Hearing aids are mass produced, incredibly expensive, and extremely inefficient. I could never force myself, however, to invest the time and effort that would be required to tackle this problem area, even though I realize how important the subject is. For some reason, the subject just doesn't send me. I hope that maybe someone else will tackle this project.

JE: As you assess your motivations for writing, do you like the fact of *having* written more than the actual process of writing itself?

JM: For me, the accomplishment is far more rewarding than the process. I hate the actual process of writing. I only write because it furnishes me a living. I don't enjoy the regimen involved with writing.

JE: Are you a disciplined writer? Do you work according to a fixed schedule? Are you able to sustain your interest in a project once you begin?

JM: Yes, I usually am. I write every morning. I get up earlier and earlier as the project progresses. My usual writing hour is around 6:00 a.m. and, as I get further into the project, I will usually get up around 5:00 a.m. This pattern developed while writing my first book. My children were young, and I had to get my writing done before they awoke at 7:30 a.m. Otherwise, I found it difficult to sit down at the typewriter and work without interruption.

JE: Do you enjoy writing at home? Are you ever bothered by the distractions of working at home?

JM: I love writing at home. For one thing, it is the only place where one doesn't have to get dressed. I like to plunk down in my dressing gown at 5:00 or 6:00 a.m., make some coffee, and start writing. In my view, that is the ideal situation. I would hate to have to get dressed and go to some foreign environment.

JE: Would you describe yourself as a "technique-conscious" writer? Is technique a major concern?

JM: Yes. I'm very much interested in technique. That's the whole point of writing. Without technique, one might as well take up another trade. I do not mean to imply that style cannot be learned; it can, and it must. I advise young writers to work hard at developing a readable style. Most textbooks argue, "Don't try to achieve style, just be yourself." I disagree with that view. When a writer submits an article or book for publication, it will be judged on the basis of agreed-upon standards. A writer cannot count on an editor to repair his prose. Indeed, I think a lot of important work is impaired because the writer is style-deaf. A good example that comes readily to mind is Ralph Nader's classic, *Unsafe At Any Speed*, which suffers seriously in this regard.

JE: Do you labor over language? Do words come easily to you?

JM: I always agonize. There's not a minute that goes by that is free of agony. I write very slowly. Words rarely flow smoothly the first time around. I rewrite most of what I write countless times. It would not be unusual for me to go through a ream of paper while working on an ordinary magazine article. My writing is full of false starts and stops, full of wrong words and phrases. I'm not especially deft when it comes to using the language. I tend to learn as I go along.

JE: To what extent is your work mapped out before you begin writing? Do you work from a well-organized outline?

JM: Basically, my work surprises me as it progresses. I am always asked, in the course of working on a book, "Have you finished the research yet?" To me, research and writing are inseparable. They are interdependent, and I do the two things simultaneously. Often, I will find huge holes in my research. When that happens, I will fill them in with luck, or whatever else I can contrive to do the job, and continue forward with the project. Research is a continuous process that cannot be divorced from writing. In my case, I am constantly doing research up until the very last minute. In fact, after a book has been released, I still find that the research is not complete. All of the above means that it is extremely difficult for me to work from a pre-conceived outline, as my work takes new shape with each new bit of relevant research.

JE: Do you aim at smaller problem areas or prefer to tackle larger areas of concern?

JM: I prefer the former. Of course, that may simply reflect my own mental laziness. I do not aspire to be a general philosopher. I would much rather knife away at a few issues as effectively as I can. If I'm going to tackle a project, I want to really dig into it. That is why I take on such a limited number of areas; I hate having to dig into a project. However, when I do dig in, I do so because the subject has somehow caught my eye. In such cases, I'm genuinely interested in rectifying the matter.

JE: Do you still get rejection slips these days and, if so, how do they affect you? .

JM: At this point, I write mostly on the basis of commission. Sometimes, though, I will initiate projects of special personal interest. Most of my early work met with repeated rejection. Obviously, I wasn't too pleased. Much to my amazement, though, the more one publishes, the easier it is to get published. One's standing rises in the most incredible manner. Editors will come knocking with all sorts of interesting projects.

JE: Do you find it difficult to motivate yourself to write, what with your many other personal interests?

JM: That's a very difficult question to answer. I feel that if one is going to write, it has to be done at the expense of one's other interests. In my case, I write every day. The discouraging thing, at least for me, is I know that whatever I've written on a given day will have to be rewritten before it's finished. As I said earlier, I disagree with the notion that writers should expect their work to be fixed by an editor. I would never dream of passing off that responsibility to him. That's an extremely irresponsible attitude, one that should be discouraged at all cost.

JE: Do you view television, as it presently functions, as a useful muckraking device? Is it living up to its responsibility in terms of educating the public in critical problem areas?

JM: I don't like television very much. I've never really acquired the habit. As a result, I probably miss all sorts of things which I would have liked. I do enjoy, though, shows like *60 Minutes*, which is an excellent program. Off hand, I cannot think of any other program I watch on a regular basis. In England, the British Broadcasting Corporation has done a great deal of significant work in the area of public education. It's really quite good!

JE: Is your celebrity status a boon when it comes to conducting research?

Does it open up doors that would otherwise remain closed?

JM: That's a most intriguing question. There is an obvious handicap in my calling up someone and saying, "Hello, this is Jessica Mitford speaking . . . ." There are various ways I've developed to get around this problem. For example, I might have someone pose as a graduate student, working on their Ph.D. dissertation or something, write or call the person in question under an assumed name. On the whole, I have found that people are incredibly easy to interview. Average citizens love to be interviewed. They're always anxious to tell you what it is they're thinking and doing. For example, undertakers are quite proud of being called "funeral directors." They masquerade as professionals who specialize in grief therapy. To perpetuate their rotten business, they relish being interviewed. It gives them an opportunity to propagandize on their own behalf.

JE: What prompted you to write *The American Way of Death*? How did the project evolve?

JM: My second husband was the inspiration behind that particular effort. He wanted to write an article on the funeral industry. As a lawyer, he represents a large number of trade union workers and various poor people. During the middle 1950s, he became outraged when he began to notice that every time the breadwinner of the family died, the widow, who was supposed to get the deceased's union insurance benefits, was left virtually penniless after paying the funeral bills. In the end, the undertaker would get the whole lot. If the gratuity was $1,000, the funeral would invariably cost $1,000; if it was $1,500, the cost would be $1,500. Somehow, the morticians would always manage to wring the money out of these widows. So I wrote an article in 1957 entitled, "St. Peter, Don't You Call Me." It was the second article I had ever published. The article led to my writing *The American Way of Death*, and served as an outline for the book.

JE: Have you found that your own activism has in any sense waned with the passage of years? Has middle age made you any more conservative in outlook?

JM: I don't think I've become more conservative, but, like everything else, I suppose my involvement has waned somewhat. The passage of years, as you point out, certainly does not enhance activism or any other aspect of life. Since leaving the Communist Party in 1958, I have primarily concentrated my energies on writing. I must admit that many of the articles I write are quite trivial. I wrote them because they amuse me. These subjects are little corners of life that I like to examine, tiny corners of the mind that I like to probe. For example, the Famous Writer's School or the funeral industry are fairly easy targets. They are quite fun to write about. These articles by no means attack imperialism at its roots. Rather than going after more pervasive evils, my nature is such that I prefer doing what I can in terms of these very miniscule areas. Of course, two of my books are quite different in this regard; *Kind and Usual Punishment: The Prison Business* and *The Trial of Dr. Spock* do attack major social issues.

JE: Can you see some evidence that your books and articles have made a difference in remedying some of the evils you've written about?

JM: Yes. Let me give you two specific examples. About five years ago, the Federal Trade Commission's Bureau of Consumer Affairs initiated a study of the entire funeral industry. Moreover, the Federal Trade Commission has just proposed a very stiff law which will, if enacted, go a long way toward curbing the deceptive practices and commercialism inherent in the funeral business. It will constitute a positive step in the right direction. Secondly, I was delighted to learn that the Famous Writer's School went bankrupt, although it now seems to be creeping back again. In both cases, I think my work might have played some small part in calling attention to these problem areas.

JE: Have you ever avoided exposing an issue or institution because it was too hot to handle or because of personal threats or reprisals?

JM: I can't think of a single one. I suppose that during the McCarthy era, I became somewhat thick-skinned. I grew accustomed to having my phone tapped and my house bugged. It never would have occured to me to back off because of government harassment. I've grown accustomed to being attacked by said government. I have no fear of retribution.

JE: In your efforts to expose particular evils of the American system, have you ever been courted by the establishment?

JM: No, not really. At any rate, I think the so-called establishment has improved in this regard. My husband and I, as well as all of our personal associates, many of whom were members of the Communist Party, were never once visited by the Federal Bureau of Investigation. I think they knew better. I've learned that if someone comes to your house uninvited, and without a warrant for your arrest, you're perfectly justified in taking a large frying pan and bashing them over the head with it. I once wrote a letter to the FBI telling them that I kept a large frying pan by my front door and that they had better "Watch out!"

JE: How do you respond to current efforts aimed at keeping such as unpopular groups, as the American Nazi Party, from organizing and demonstrating against those issues that concern them?

JM: I know the whole scope of that argument, from the views of the American Civil Liberties Union to the views of the various other groups concerned. Unfortunately, my gut reaction is that no special efforts should be made to protect the civil rights of that group. In my view, it is a stupid disgrace that the ACLU is expending so much time and energy in Mississippi protecting the Ku Klux Klan. It is all so inane! Why can't the ACLU spend the same effort protecting the rights of blacks? As I pointed out in *A Fine Old Conflict*, I've never belonged to the ACLU. I bitterly resented their attitude during the whole Cold War era, and still do. Although I have worked closely with the ACLU on occasion, and have undertaken projects at their request, I have very queasy feelings about the group. They're not my kind of people; they're just too wishy washy. Actually some of their members are delightful individuals. However, I find the ACLU's whole liberal stance most distressing and boring. As a result, I've never joined the organization.

JE: How do you feel about people, such as actress Jane Fonda, who direct their protests at big business, corporations like Dow Chemical?

JM: I've known Jane Fonda, on and off, for several years. She spoke at a fundraiser conducted by an organization that I helped sponsor. I found her extremely intelligent and quite sincere. She is not a bit like the traditional Hollywood movie-star type. When we first met at this fundraiser, she gave me a huge file of correspondence from various prison inmates. At the time, Jane was terribly involved with the issue of prison reform. I was then working on my prison expose and quite interested in those letters and in visiting correctional institutions. I, too, am very much concerned, as is Jane Fonda, with combatting the excesses of big business and eliminating those vestiges of exploitation which exist.

JE: In the course of conducting your research on the American correctional system, did you have an opportunity to meet with prison inmates or visit the institutions on a first-hand basis?

JM: Almost every Department of Corrections has denied my repeated requests to be allowed to visit inside our prison system. These refusals have been based on the contention that convicts are just too dangerous and so forth, or more astoundingly, that my visit would violate the prisoner's right of privacy. It was all so lovely, because, you see, the fact is that prisoners have no right of privacy. So I initiated lawsuits all across the country; I had about five or six of them going at one time. Finally, the Supreme Court ruled against my petitions. It seemed that reporters have no right to visit within our corrections system.

JE: Are there other problem areas that interest you—problems that you hope to pursue in the future?

JM: None. I hate pursuing anything. In most cases, I would much rather rest at home than write. When something comes my way or particularly strikes me, I will do something about it. That may be a self-indulgent attitude, but, on the other hand, I don't do good work unless I'm really fascinated, even momentarily, by the subject. Over the last twenty years or so, I've been asked, on numerous occasions, what project I might tackle next. My answer is always the same: I never know.

JE: Does writing serve a cathartic value for you—that is, does it encourage self-examination and greater self-awareness?

JM: I'm not really sure. I wish I could claim such depth. I think one always experiences some degree of personal growth during the process of writing. How much, though, I don't quite know. The book that comes the closest to fulfilling that hope is *Daughters and Rebels*, my first effort.

JE: To what extent is your work influenced by the perceptions of the critics? Do their views play a large role in what you write?

JM: Well, it all depends on the critic in question. If I admire the critic, then, yes, I would be affected by the review. I would be shattered if he disliked a book of mine. However, if I don't admire the critic, then his assessment would count very little with me. It would register no real impact.

JE: What kind of reader response gives you the greatest personal satisfaction?

JM: I'm most affected by those readers who write and tell me that my work struck a responsive chord in them. For example, I can't begin to tell you how many hundreds of letters I received with the publication of my book, *The American Way of Death*. My house was literally filled with marvelous letters from all kinds of people. I was determined to answer each of the letters personally. Finally, I was forced to hire a young girl to help me with the flood of correspondence. It was overwhelming!

JE: Do you like being described as a "muckraker?" Is it a role that suits you?

JM: Yes, I think so. Otherwise, I would probably be writing very different kinds of things. Actually, I look forward to tackling a big industry that is obviously powerful and influential, particularly when that industry wields its power in a destructive manner. Yes, I enjoy "crossing swords" with these characters. Hopefully, it does some good.

JE: Finally, what projects do you currently have on tap?

JM: I am now in the process of promoting my new book, *Poison Penmanship: The Gentle Art of Muckraking*. It comprises a collection of articles I've written over the last twenty years. The articles, which were all previously published in various magazines, each have an introductory note or comment on how that particular article came about. The book explains the behind-the-scenes aspects of modern muckraking. It includes such topics as: how I gathered source materials, how these particular investigations were conducted, where the ideas for the articles originated, and what mistakes were made in the process. It is ostensibly a how-to-do-it book, showing the development of my methods and techniques. Basically, my objective in writing the book was to share my trial-

and-error experiments as a muckraker, and assist others who might like to follow along similar lines.

Richard Arm

Richard Armour: Humor Is His Shield: Satire Is His Spear

BACK-TO-NATURE-WRITER

In books and articles he hymns the pleasures
Of simple, golden days of long ago
He quotes at length, and obviously treasures,
Bucolic thoughts of Wordsworth and Thoreau.

He sometimes grieves, he sometimes shouts defiance
At man too mechanized, enthralled with chrome.
Deploring deeds of industry and science,
He writes of rustic woodlands as his home.

But do not shed for him a tear of pity
Or hasten by his written word to judge him.
He lives where born, amidst a bustling city
From which a team of horses couldn't budge him.

———Richard Armour

Richard Armour, one of America's most celebrated writers of humorous and whimsical prose, has made a distinguised mark on contemporary literature. Armour, a former professor of English at many colleges and universities—most recently at Scripps College and the Claremont Graduate School—has written over 6,000 articles and pieces of light verse for a wide variety of publications. In addition, he has authored fifty-six books, including such best-selling works as *It All Started with Columbus, Twisted Tales from Shakespeare, The Classics Reclassified, Golf is a Four-Letter Word*, and *Through Darkest Adolescence*. Armour's books has sold over a million copies in this country and have been translated into many languages.

Armour's first book of humor—*Yours for the Asking*—was published in 1942. It was a collection of the author's favorite light verse drawn mostly from the pages of *The New Yorker*. Since the publication of that first book, Armour has gone on to pen humor and satire for the past forty years. During most of that time, he has been considered one of the stellar talents in his particular field by virtually all the experts *save one!*

The exception, of course, is Armour himself. Despite his myriad contributions to the genre, Armour hesitates to call himself a major writer, much less a great one. In a recent conversation on this subject, I asked Armour why he refuses to classifty himself with the great writers he esteems. He replied: "Alas, I wish I could write a successful novel or a full-length play. I also wish I were better at writing satire. However, there is a cowardly streak in me, a desire to be liked, that makes me a rather soft satirist except for a few of my books and articles. No, I am not one of the 'great' writers, but, fortunately, I have found my own niche, in which I have worked for forty years with some success. I leave the great works of fiction and drama to others."

Known primarily as a humorist and satirist, Armour has not always written in these areas. His first three books were big, serious, "publish-or-perish" volumes. It was not until he had been out of college for ten years that he discovered his ability to write humor. In the summer of 1937, he sent a piece of light verse to *The New Yorker* and one to *The Saturday Evening Post*. He sold both of them, and from that moment felt he could write something editors would want and readers would read. Had both pieces been returned with rejection slips, as he now admits, he might have quit right then and never known what he could do. Fortunately for his readers, those two pieces were accepted, laying the foundation for the thousands which followed.

Despite numerous successes, and persistent critical acclaim, Armour harbors serious doubts about his future. The author puts it this way: "Age is good for wine and cheese, and a certain amount of it is good for a writer. It takes time to store the mind with experiences, ideas, and words. But age has its drawbacks, especially for a writer of humor and satire. While writers of serious poetry and fiction can still do good work in their eighties, writers of humor usually begin to fade by the time they are seventy, if not earlier. Since I am seventy, this is something often on my mind. This decline, or even cessation, is, I think, because humor and satire at their best require alertness, sharpness, and daring to experiment with new situations. Like sight and hearing, these diminish with time. We have glasses to improve our sight, and hearing aids to help our hearing. What I need, at seventy, is a device I can attach to my brain that will sharpen my thinking. Maybe some day, but too late for me, one can get not only a heart transplant but a brain transplant. Meanwhile, I do the best I can with my weakening old brain. It has served me well for all these years, and I am grateful for it. I can still detect the absurd and incongruous, and sometimes my old brain amazes me. I occasionally write something that even an editor thinks is as good as anything I have ever done before. More often though, I read something I wrote thirty or forty years ago and wonder how I ever did it. I think the imagination, which is important in humor and satire, as well as in all creative work, is at its height in children. This gives me something to look forward to: second childhood. I may have another spurt of good writing then, if I have the strength to hit the typewriter keys. By the way, it just occurs to me how grateful I should be that the typewriter keys do not hit back."

Author Richard Armour lives in Claremont, California, in a picturesque Japanese-looking home, which was built in 1963 after he and his family lived for five years in a Zen Buddhist temple in Kyoto, Japan. On a bright, warm day in his cluttered study, Armour talked lovingly about his craft and his hopes for his work, giving the reader a first-hand insight into this extraordinary writer and the magic which sustains his work, a magic which has brought joy and pleasure to the millions of readers who cherish his books and revere him as one of America's greatest living humorists.

*   *   *   *   *

JE: Can you say how you started writing humor?

RA: When I was in high school, I wrote some serious, sentimental poetry. It was the only writing I did, apart from assigned papers. Happily, I got that so-called poetry out of my system and wrote no more of it. In college (Pomona College), I did all kinds of writing—for the college paper, the literary magazine, the yearbook, and—yes, the humor magazine. For the campus humor magazine, I wrote both verse and prose, and that was where my humor was first published. I kept none of it, and so, mercifully, don't know how bad it probably was.

But my sharpest and bawdiest humor was written for my college friends, and was about our professors. Had these professors ever seen some of it, I would never have graduated. I would have been thrown out—or thrown up. I have never since written humor or satire with the wickedness of some lines I wrote about a certain professor of mathematics. Mathematics, of course, was my weakest field, and it produced my strongest, meanest writing. At alumni gatherings, I have often encountered a classmate who could quote all of the lines, although I can remember only a few. Apparently, it was a piece of humor that appealed to the adolescent mind. It may have been a classic, but it wasn't for a class, at least not when the professor (a good man, I am sure) was around. In graduate school, at Harvard, where I took a Ph.D. in English philology, I was too frightened to write any humor. The same was true when I was a young instructor at the University of Texas and Northwestern University. But after I had written two "publish-or-perish" books and was working on a third, *Coleridge the Talker* (in collaboration with Raymond F. Howes), a book published in 1940 that is still in print, I was well enough established academically to write for fun. I was then teaching at Wells College, in upstate New York, and I remember what started my writing of humor. It was in the summer of 1937. My wife was away, visiting her family in California, and I was invited to a picnic by some friends who thought I must be lonesome (I was). It was that picnic, on the edge of Lake Cayuga, that caused me to write "Charm for a Picnic," which I sent to *The Saturday Evening Post*. Miracle of miracles, it was accepted, a playful, home-and-family piece of light verse. Within a few days, I wrote a somewhat more sophisticated piece of light verse, and sent it to *The New Yorker*, which accepted it. So I sold the first two bits (and for more than two bits) of light verse I submitted to editors. It was a little like making two holes-in-one on a golfer's first time on the tee. Now I knew I could do it, and I kept writing—first light verse and then prose humor—every day. If those first pieces had come back, I would probably have quit, thinking writing, or writing of humor, was not for me.

JE: Why did you choose humor as a means of self-expression?

RA: I suppose that humor, the observation of the imperfections, incongruities, and stupidities of the human race, was latent in me. Perhaps I inherited it from my father's side of the family. My father wrote occasional light verse, but never tried to publish any. He wrote it for birthdays, anniversaries, and the like. My uncle Lester was the town jester, well known for his practical jokes. It is a help for a writer of humor to have oddball relatives, and I had them in abundance. They are all to be found in *Drug Store Days*, my own favorite of my fifty-six books. But in that book and others, I made fun more of myself than of others. I have never forgotten the words of an eighteenth-century physician, in a letter to his son, who was about to make his way in the world. The words that have stuck with me are: "He is never laughed at who laughs at himself first." I have made fun of myself, made a fool of myself, for so many years that it now comes easily. In the same way, I found how important it was to say, "I'm sorry." Now, I say it automatically. If I bump into a tree, I say "I'm sorry" to the tree. Humor, having fun with the oddities of the human race, to which I think I belong, is now second nature to me. Come to think of it, I don't know what my first nature is. Since I am fairly thin-skinned, I don't like to be laughed at. So I notice what is laughable about me, and beat others to the punch, or to the punch-line. My readers seem to enjoy that, and I enjoy being enjoyed.

JE: Has your work, to this point, lived up to your expectations?

RA: Dickens wrote *Great Expectations*. Cued by a word, if I wrote about the Old West, the West of the Frontier, when men (and not just baseball players) chewed tobacco and kept a spittoon handy, I would like to do a book entitled *Great Expectorations*. My work probably fulfills my expectorations; at least some critics think so. But I have far higher goals than I have ever achieved, or come anywhere near achieving. I wish, for one thing, I were about thirty years younger and thirty times more talented. Then I might try to write a new *Gulliver's Travels* or *Candide*. I should like to be more than a folksy humorist. I should like to be a razor-edged satirist. A humorist entertains his readers. A satirist makes them think. A satirist is more cerebral. Obviously, I have models, writers I admire. I wish I could get at least into their neighborhood—which would mean a large move indeed. Swift and Voltaire are two of the writers I not only admire but occasionally imitate. My *It All Started with Stones and Clubs* is a Swiftian satire on the history of war and weaponry. Its technique is irony—saying one thing and meaning another. It is a world apart from my light verse and most of my prose books. But my imitation of Swift can be found also in the last chapter of *Going Around in Academic Circles*, called "How to Burn a Book." In other works, such as *The Academic Bestiary*, probably the sharpest of my three satirical books about education, the reader may see a hint of Voltaire. In still other books, for instance *Through Darkest Adolescence* and *The Happy Bookers*, a playful history of librarians and their world (manuscripts, books, libraries), I have gone my own way. Perhaps I have blazed a few trails, though not an arsonist.

JE: To what extent is your work autobiographical?

RA: Anyone who has read either my light verse or my prose should know me quite well. I am there, writing about myself, my family, my friends, and the foolish things that are universal. I suppose what the reader learns most about me is that I am a lover of words. Much of this goes back to that work in English philology at Harvard. Work is a four-letter word, but a good word. I work surrounded by dictionaries, and always look up not only the meaning and pronunciation, but the etymology of words. Once I wrote an article for *The Journal of the American Medical Association* about the word "medicine." Doctors have too much else to do than to learn, for instance, that in the Middle Ages one whom we would call a quack was called a "medicaster." And I wrote an article for another journal about the ship's distress signal, May Day. It has nothing to do with either May or Day, but derives from the French *m'aider*, meaning help me. But readers also learn about my wife and children in *My Life With Women*, about how my service in the Army improved my writing in *It All Started with Freshman English*, and so on. By the way, after serving with antiaircraft artillery troops for two years in World War II, I trailed a general, whose aide I had become, to the War Department General Staff. There, among other duties, I was a ghost writer for, first, General Marshall, and then General Eisenhower, helping the Chief of Staff with speeches, letters, and other word chores. My light verse, collected in *Light Armour*, *Nights with Armour*, *The Spouse in the House*, and other books is almost all personal and revealing—and I hope universal. I am just a specimen.

JE: Which writers have most influenced your development as a humorist?

RA: I have already told you a few of the writers who have influenced me. But these influenced my prose books. There is another group of writers who were my models for light verse. These include Phyllis McGinley (who wrote the introduction to my *For Partly Proud Parents*), Odgen Nash (who wrote the foreword to my *On Your Marks: A Package of Punctuation*, which was made into an animated educational film that won second place at the American Film Festival in 1971), David McCord, Morris Bishop, Arthur Guiterman, and Samuel Hoffenstein. By the way, Everett S. Allen's *Famous American Humorous*

Poets, published in 1968, includes chapters about thirteen writers of humorous poetry (or light verse), going back a hundred years. I, miraculously, am one of them, and the only one still writing.

JE: How much of your work is rooted in personal experience?

RA: Virtually all of my light verse is based on personal experience, or what I have observed. Some of my books of prose are based on personal experience, while others are based on my experience as a longtime professor and dean of the faculty in a wide variety of colleges and universities. Though I was a Professor of English, which would explain my *Twisted Tales from Shakespeare*, *English Lit Relit, American Lit Relit*, etc., I wrote many books that were parodies of history, such as *It All Started with Columbus* (now updated to the present, after Watergate, and retitled *It All Would Have Startled Columbus*), *It All Started with Europa, It All Started with Marx* (which keeps me and my books out of the Soviet Union), and many others. During 1964 to 1970, when I lectured in Europe and Asia for the State Department, most of my reading was in history and political science. In fact, a book a little earlier than that, *Our Presidents*, was based on reading in history and picking the brains of my American history colleagues.

JE: What kinds of situations do you most like to draw on in terms of subject matter?

RA: Except for the prose books, which probe more deeply into a subject, I enjoy most the everyday happenings in our family, with our neighbors, and with ordinary people, of which I am one. I often get ideas when driving, when gardening, when eating. This is the universal material out of which virtually all of my light verse and some of my prose articles and books are made.

JE: Do you tailor your work to fit a particular audience?

RA: What I like best is when an editor writes or phones me and asks for a poem or an article on a specific subject. The idea and the market come together. All I have to do is a little thinking and writing and revising. Then I know what I have written is sold. It is much harder to think up an idea and a market. But this, which is called freelancing (and it is often the author who is lanced), is what I do every day. Over the years, I have come to know the markets pretty well. But new magazines come on the scene, old ones fade away, and often there is a change of editors, which may change the nature of the market. I wrote articles for *Playboy* for many years and am included in half a dozen *Playboy* anthologies. But a new editor came along (not Hefner, who is the Publisher), and I have had no luck with him whatsoever, and have quit trying. It is helpful, perhaps necessary, to have a certain market in mind. It would be foolish, for example, to write a *Good Housekeeping* sort of piece and send it to *Penthouse*. The only thing they have in common is "house"—and a house is not a home. However, I like to write something that might be used by any one of several magazines. Otherwise, if the magazine toward which it was slanted doesn't take it, the piece is dead. I think of magazines not singly, but in groups.

JE: How important an ingredient do you consider technique in writing humor?

RA: Technique is important in writing of all kinds, but probably most important in writing humor and satire (perhaps most of all in writing light verse). The serious poet has lofty thoughts, lyricism, imagery. Lacking these, the light verse writer goes in for technique—variety of metrical patterns, unusual rhymes, and the like. So much emphasis on technique would never be used by a serious poet, since it would draw the reader away from the thought and other poetic qualities. In humor, generally, technique is more important than in writing of other kinds. This involves playing with words, for instance. I dislike the work "pun," an ugly, blunt little word. It comes from the Italian *puntiglio*, a small point or a quibble. I prefer "word play," which correctly describes it and is used in the French *jeu de mots* and the German *wortspiel*. By the way, on the distinction between poetry and prose, I have always liked Coleridge's emphasis on words in his "Prose is words in their best order; poetry is the best words in their best order." This is not the whole story of the difference between poetry and prose, but it is an important part of it. Two modern writers who play brilliantly with words in their prose humor are S. J. Perelman and Peter DeVries. Especially noteworthy are the opening paragraphs of Perelman's books.

JE: Do you write every day or only under inspiration?

RA: I write every day, whenever I find some spare minutes. I read fast, I write fast, and I forget fast. As for inspiration, I think you have to go after it, not wait for it to come. You know the old saying about writing being 10 percent inspiration and 90 percent perspiration. Well, I would add, and give a high percentage to, a third element: desperation. That's what I have, desperation—fear that I'm washed up, can't get another idea, won't place another book, article, or poem. Such moments or hours usually come just before a good and profitable period of production.

JE: How far removed must you be from your subject in order to write humor?

RA: Wordsworth wrote of "emotion recollected in tranquility." Most of the great writing, I suppose, is of that kind. But I think humor can draw upon past experience or equally well on the present. Perhaps humor is less emotional and more intellectual or rational than most think. Phyllis McGinley, the only light verse writer to win the Pulitzer Prize for poetry, once commented that light verse is more intellectual than poetry. Humor does, indeed, involve thinking more than feeling. Satire involves feeling strongly about something and then writing about it coldly, rationally, but with imagination, of course. *Gulliver's Travels* has all of these qualities, and so does *Huckleberry Finn*, my favorite American novel. One reason it is my favorite is that it can be read again and again, each time finding new meanings as well as new applications of events and feelings of the past to the present. The best humor is not obvious. It brings not a belly laugh, but a smile or a feeling of understanding and satisfaction. Laughter, by the way, has been defined as "feeling good all over and showing it in one place." On the psychology of humor, I would recommend Harvey Mindess's *Laughter and Liberation*. Mindess is a practicing psychologist, and he brings me into one chapter of the book.

JE: Is the act of writing easy for you? Do you enjoy the process of writing itself?

RA: Writing is hard work and never gets easier. The reason it doesn't get easier, at least for me, is my trying to excel, or even to equal, what I wrote many years ago. I wonder, now, that I ever could have had the total recall it took to write *Drug Store Days* or the knowledge of Shakespeare to write *Twisted Tales from Shakespeare*. It is hard enough to keep going, after more than forty years of writing, but harder still to improve or to hold one's own.

JE: How necessary is it that the reader see himself in your humor?

RA: If the reader doesn't see himself, or recognize himself, he should see his friends or enemies or casual acquaintances. In other words, he should recognize that the writer is writing about the human race, and he is of that race. Whether it is an endangered race perhaps depends on the existence and the activity of self-critical humor. I think the sense of humor is a sixth sense. Everyone is born with it, but, like muscle, it can atrophy from lack of use, just as it can grow with use. To "Be thyself," I suppose we could add "See thyself."

The only book I have written that has offended some readers is *Through Darkest Adolescence*. Those it has offended are unwilling to identify with the strange creatures (modeled on our son and daughter, then adolescents) about whom I write. But, happily, they are a small minority. It is probably my son and daughter's favorite of my books. In fact, it may be the only one of my books they have read through.

JE: Has your writing improved significantly with the passage of time? Can you detect clear signs of growth and maturation?

RA: In some ways, I suppose, my work has improved. I know the nuances of technique better. I am more cautious and selective in the use of word play. But in more ways my work has declined. I haven't the imagination, the originality, or the stamina I had thirty years ago, or even ten years ago. In youth, imagination and memory are at their best. Both of these decline with the passing of years. Technique improves, and an older writer must therefore make all possible use of it. I don't know the exact age at which imagination, memory, and technique are nearest to their best. I do know what I have lost and what I have gained, and I lament the loss more than I rejoice about the gain.

JE: Is simplicity an important element in writing humor? How necessary is it to draw on basic life situations?

RA: Simplicity is important in all forms of writing—even a letter or a report. It may be more important in humor than in other kinds of writing. After all, the reader doesn't expect to have to labor his way through a book or an article of humor. It isn't easy to write humor in any fashion, but what is important is that the traces of work be brushed aside or hidden. Humor should look easy. Referring to word play again, I would say that this is at its worst when it laboriously makes its way to the high point, or just to the point. A good source here is Bennett Cerf's *Treasury of Atrocious Puns*. What makes them atrocious is the evidence of effort, the long build-up to not much of a conclusion.

JE: What hopes do you have for your work in terms of impact?

RA: I hope my light verse and prose humor has given and will continue to give pleasure and help erase pain. As for my prose satire, I hope it causes some thinking about such things as man's selfishness, man's vanity, man's inhumanity to man. But all I can do is hope. I cannot be sure.

JE: How much of the child in you surfaces in your humor? What about the adult in you?

RA: I have long thought that one of the strengths of the young, along with imagination and memory, is a lively sense of humor. Young people enjoy humor of all kinds, from *Mad* magazine to Thurber. As people get older, they begin to specialize in the humor they like, just as they specialize in other things. The child in me is quick to catch absurdities, things out of kilter. One of my dozen books for children, *The Strange Dreams of Rover Jones*, in which the roles of a dog and his master are reversed, came out of my childishness, I suppose, but I am not sure whether it was first childhood or second childhood. Writing books for children has shown me that it is possible to write humor that children can enjoy—and some adults can enjoy also. The adult in me surfaces in my light verse about age and about current experiences. It makes me more than ever want to be, and be known as, a satirist, which is something very adult. But in much humor, especially such humor as mine, the child and the adult are together, perhaps one predominant one day and the other the next. I have tried hard to break through the generation gap, to write for all ages. This is true, for example, in *Our Presidents* and *Sea Full of Whales*.

JE: As you see it, what qualities make for a good humorist?

RA: A good humorist is born—and made better. A humorist has such qualities as love of words, willingness to make fun of himself, and constant observations of the doings and undoings of the human race.

JE: To what extent do you turn to humor as a means to cope with your own life circumstances?

RA: Humor has helped me greatly in my own life, especially my domestic life, the family and home. I have written lightly about everything in our home in *Armour's Armoury*, the verse feature that appears weekly in *Family Weekly* in more than 350 newspapers. This brings me much response, and shows that the things that irritate me irritate others, and can best be handled by being exposed and laughed at. I once wrote an article for *Parents' Magazine* called "Humor to the Rescue," that told of some specific tangles in our household and how humor untangled them.

JE: Do you have to work to be humorous, or does it come naturally in your thoughts and actions?

RA: Over the years, I have trained myself to look for material to be written about humorously. One source is the daily newspaper. Another is the host-guest relationship. Still another is our neighbors, and so on. So I think humor comes more naturally now, or I know better where to look for it. I got two articles out of our neighbor's oak tree's leaves, which, helped by the prevailing winds, constantly have to be raked up in our yard. One article, I remember, was called "Leaf Me Alone."

JE: Are there certain subjects which lend themselves more to humor than others?

RA: There is the basic material for a humorous piece of verse or a humorous article, maybe even a book, in human relations—relations of man to man, or woman to woman, or man to woman. Women, the opposite sex, are a special source of humorous material for me. This is true mostly in my light verse, where I am constantly writing about the battle of the sexes, which I think is about over, and I know who won. It is also present in such different books as *The Spouse in the House* (light verse, home and family themes) and *It All Started with Eve* (prose humor, famous women of history, from Eve to Mata Hari).

JE: What makes some things humorous and other things not?

RA: Everything that is capable of showing its weaknesses, which it tries to hide, everything that is widely known, is possible as material for writing humor. I have even thought of writing a humorous version of the *Old Testament*, though I would leave the *New Testament* alone. I draw the line in several places, and one has to do with a person's faith or religion. But the *Old Testament* is history, and it has possibilities. The first two chapters of *It All Started with Eve* are humorous treatments of two Biblical women, Eve and Delilah.

JE: Do you still laugh at your own work or does the process of writing diminish the pleasure you derive from reading it?

RA: I seldom reread a book of mine. The last reading is when I read page proofs. Sadly, there are two typographical errors, in of all books, *It All Started with Freshman English*. I sneak into bookstores and correct them with a pen. The reason for the errors, which I caught at once, was that my publishers thought they would save expense and also get the book out earlier if they didn't send me page proofs. Never again.

JE: To what extent does one have to have experienced pain in order to appreciate humor?

RA: I doubt that it is necessary to have experienced pain in order to appreciate humor. But humor will alleviate pain, or shift the reader's attention away from pain. I get many letters from readers who tell of being hospitalized and finding relief by reading some of my books. *The Medical Muse* and *It All Started with Hippocrates* will help either a patient or a physician. *The Medical Muse* is light verse on medical matters that appeared in a half-page feature I wrote for twenty-three years for *Postgraduate Medicine.* The Foreword was written by Dr. Charles W. Mayo, then head of the Mayo Clinic. *It All Started with Hippocrates* is a playful-factual history of medicine that was well received by the top medical historians. Both books make patients more patient, doctors tell me.

JE: What are people really laughing at when they laugh at your work?

RA: They are laughing at ridiculous twisting of facts or playing with words. Or they are laughing at what they recognize to be themselves.

JE: Do people like to admit that they exist in the context of your humor?

RA: Most are generous enough to recognize they are being made fun of. But they know that so are millions of others. My only trouble, as I mentioned earlier, has been with a few adolescents who, perhaps because they are going through what I take up clinically as a disease, are in no condition to join in the fun.

JE: Does humor have staying power or do people tend to read it once, chuckle over it, and then dismiss it?

RA: The best humor, like the best writing of any kind, can be recommended to friends and read over and over. But unless it is really very good, once is enough for most readers. However, a book of humor that hasn't been read for many years can bring laughs and smiles again. And, by the way, it is as hard to make readers laugh as it is to make them cry. Comedy is as hard to create as tragedy.

JE: When you read humor, what do you read it for?

RA: I read humor for relaxation and relief from the woes of the world, even for a short while. But as a writer of humor, I also read it to study the style and how the material is handled. I review many books of humor, and this causes me to analyze and evaluate the humor books I am assigned. I try to estimate what the effect will be on those who might be thinking of buying the book.

JE: What gives you the greatest satisfaction as a humorist?

RA: The greatest satisfaction I get as a writer of humor is to know that many readers, and I hope many critics, will understand and enjoy what I have written. Though it takes valuable time and almost as valuable postage, I am heartened by letters from happy readers, and respond at once. I am somewhat of a manic-depressive. Indeed, most writers of humor I have known have been rather depressed types. It gives me at least temporary relief from depression to know that someone likes what I have written.

JE: Do you believe that humor has the power to change, to reform, to alter attitudes, values, prejudices, etc.?

RA: Humor, but especially satire, has great power to work on prejudices and to bring about reform. A prime example on television, of course, is *All in the Family.* But *Huckleberry Finn* and many other books of humor and more than humor can alter the reader's thinking about racial prejudice, hypocrisy, and other human faults that still plague us.

JE: How do you explain the phenomenal success of popular writers such as Erma Bombeck or Sam Levenson, who write light humor?

RA: A writer like Bombeck or Levenson hits home at home, plays with everyday annoyances. This is humor, not satire. Just as Erma Bombeck has reached a large readership through her syndicated column of household humor, Art Buchwald is widely read in his column of political satire. Erma Bombeck should annoy no one. Buchwald may ruffle some feathers. We need both kinds, along with the cartoonists, amidst the daily newspaper's accounts of crime and disaster.

JE: Do you strive to be topical in your humor? Do you draw heavily on the daily news for subject inspiration?

RA: The newspaper is one of my best sources of material for both humor and satire. It is a mirror that reflects the imperfections of the human race. Sometimes, I think it is most useful after it has been read—to start a fire in the fireplace or line the bottom of a bird cage. I take our newspapers next door, where our neighbor ties them up in bales and hauls them away for recycling. This is the same neighbor whose oak leaves are such a bother, but also such good material for humor. For more than thirty years, I have written for *Quote* a piece of light verse each week, based on a news item (or news peg) which I quote before writing four stanzas in which I toy with the subject. It takes much reading of newspapers (we take three) to find such items. They should not be funny themselves, but give me something out of which to milk some humor. Finding the right item is harder than writing the sixteen lines. As I think I mentioned, that first piece of light verse I sold to *The New Yorker* in 1937 was based on a news item. However, there has been no light verse in *The New Yorker* for a long while. Ogden Nash wrote me, shortly before his death in 1971, that the last five poems he sent them had been returned. Now, the so-called poetry is often prose set up to look like poetry, and the humor is mostly in the cartoons.

JE: Is humor an effective vehicle for dealing with anger, bitterness, cynicism, and other emotions of this kind?

RA: Humor is effective in dealing with all such emotions. It depends, though, on whether it is healthy humor or what was once referred to as "sick humor." I prefer healthy humor to sick humor, and I notice that most of the so-called sick humor writers have disappeared. Perhaps they are no longer alive, or are in hospitals.

JE: Do you ever use your work as a forum from which to espouse your own social and political preferences.

RA: When humor gets into such matters as politics, it may go over into satire. I wrote what might be called political satire every week for more than twenty years for a New York paper. Though the paper had a reputation for a particular political view, I tried to be "even-handed." I found follies in my own political party as much as in the opposing political party, in my own country as well as other countries. A selection of my satirical pieces was brought together in a book called *Leading with My Left*, with an introduction by Max Eastman. I was pleased with the introduction because Eastman was the author of *Enjoyment of Laughter*, a classic on humor. Also, Eastman, as he tells in his autobiography, went all the way from a Trotsky follower, indeed the official translator of Trotsky, to a supporter of William Buckley and one of the early contributors to Buckley's *National Review*.

JE: What do you see as your basic strengths as a writer of humor? Your basic weaknesses?

RA: If I have any basic strength as a humorist, it is in the variety of subjects I have written about and the variety of literary forms I have used. I write in prose and in verse, for adults and for children, and on subjects from paleontology to art and from ceteology to sex. My *A Short History of Sex* is a clean book, but, I am happy to say, is being read by a lot of dirty-minded people. It began as an article in the *National Lampoon*. But maybe I have more quantity than quality. That might be my weakness, along with a propensity for puns or word play that I have to fight against. I have some books without a single pun, and some, I fear, with too many.

JE: Do you view yourself as an educator as well as an entertainer?

RA: My largest readership is among students. Often teachers bring a book of mine in history or literature into the classroom to lighten up a dull day. Then the students ask about the book and get it, and, I hope, are caught by the Armour habit. I think there is what I call the "hook of humor." Many students write me and thank me because they remembered something from one of my humorous books that they couldn't remember from their textbooks. Also, I have found that it is the better student who enjoys me most, and have said that if there were an H.Q., or humor quotient, it would be very close to the I.Q. In the fifty or so articles I have written in the past five years for the Education section of *The Christian Science Monitor*, I have combined lightness with seriousness and have had a gratifying response. So, in one way or another, on top of over fifty years of studying, teaching, deaning, and trusteeing in colleges, universities and graduate schools, I have tried to make a contribution to education. As I tell in *It All Started with Freshman English*, during my years of teaching I increasingly made use of humor in the classroom by writing parodies of the authors we were studying. But the students had to know an author's work well before understanding and enjoying the parody.

JE: Does a humorist fall easily into cliches? Is it hard to be original on a regular basis?

RA: Most humorists, like most serious writers, develop a recognizable style. I have tried for variety and range, and always hope to make the next book different. But it isn't all bad to have a brand of sorts and to have one's own style. It isn't easy to be fresh and original, but I make a try at it with each piece of writing.

JE: To what extent do you study humor, research humor, analyze humor, and read other writers' humor?

RA: Over the years, I have read a great many books about humor and have read, and often written reviews of, the works of contemporary humorists in prose and verse. A writer of humor, as of anything else, has to know what is going on, who his competitors are. At a number of colleges and universities, I have taken over classes in humor. Once it was a course in psychology—the psychology of humor. But more often the courses have been in American humor. I am especially interested in the writers of humor in the 1930s, during the worst period of the Depression. That was the Golden Age of American humor, the time of such writers as Thurber, Benchley, and Dorothy Parker; Fred Allen on the radio, Laurel and Hardy, Chaplin, Buster Keaton, and others in the movies. American humor seems to have hit its high points during difficult times—the Revolution, the Frontier movement, the Civil War, and the Depression. It makes me think there is a connection betwen hardship and humor. Humor seems to be a Godgiven gift that sees us through the difficult times. Maybe all we need now for humor to get better is for times to get worse.

JE: What are the major pitfalls when it comes to writing humor? What are the key things to avoid?

RA: There are no more pitfalls, or pratfalls, in writing humor than in writing anything else. It's a matter of reading the best writers in the field, studying yourself and those around you for humorous material, and writing, or trying to write, every day. Oh yes, and keeping a dictionary close at hand. Some are concerned that if they read and in any way imitate other writers they will be guilty of plagiarism. But remember Robert Louis Stevenson's saying he "played the sedulous ape" to writers he named. One's own character and personality soon take over, and one will write in one's own way, guided and spurred by the writers of humor who have been read. But I have written about all such things in the only how-to book on the subject, *Writing Light Verse and Prose Humor*.

JE: What criteria do you use to determine whether something is really humorous?

RA: To find out whether something I have written is humorous is very simple. I try it on my wife. If I get her approval, which isn't easy, what I have written is all right. She is tougher on me than any editor.

JE: What are the primary difficulties you've encountered in developing your own brand of humor?

RA: I don't know of any special difficulties I have had. Or, if I have had them, I overcame them with the desperation I mentioned earlier. A style or brand of humor gradually comes into being as the result of reading, observing, writing, and rewriting. In addition to my wife, who is inclined to be negative, I have had a few editors—really only two—who were both critical and creative. If I had difficulties, if I was not doing my best, they would push me out of the rut. I wish there were more editors like these two, but they seem to be rare. At the moment, alas, I have neither one.

JE: How do you explain your attraction to writing humor these days? What challenges does it represent?

RA: It's not that I'm especially attracted to writing humor. Humor in short form, from a quatrain of light verse for a magazine to a book of not more than 150 pages, is all I have written and all I seem able to write. I envy writers like James Michener and Irving Stone, with their massive fact-fiction books that are invariably best sellers. I would trade ten of my books, or all of my books, for one of theirs. But I know my abilities and I know my limits. I'll just go on writing humor in prose and verse, for children and for adults. I am a minor writer, and I'll keep mining. The challenge, regardless of tastes of the times, is to write humor that will be read and, I hope, will be enjoyed.

JE: In what ways have you attempted to expand the parameters of your work?

RA: My humor is already wide in scope—in subjects and in techniques. What I need is probably more depth, more polish. When I am started on a book, I am wild to push on with it and to finish it. In one way, and in only one way, I am like Byron. "I write as the tiger leaps," he once said. I write that way too but I am not a lionized tiger. I do not leap on my prey, but leap just as a way of keeping busy and getting through with the task at hand.

JE: How precarious is the life of a humorist—that is, is there the constant fear of drying up in terms of new ideas?

RA: Of course, I am always afraid of drying up. I think each piece of writing, whether a humorous poem or a book of humor or satire, will be my last. Then comes a phone call or a letter that gives me an idea, a project. And I start that leaping again. It can't go on forever, of course, but I'd like a few more years of productivity.

JE: In writing humor, how do you avoid the trap of becoming preachy or polemical?

RA: Preachiness and humor don't mix. They are at opposite poles. I have no worry about becoming preachy. The nearest I get to preachiness is when I am near our preacher. But as I sit in our pew on Sunday, I soon pull out my notebook and start scribbling. I am a favorite of our preacher's. He thinks I am taking notes on his sermon.

JE: Do you consciously write your humor on more than one level? Are there hidden messages in your work?

RA: Yes, I write humor on several levels. One level is in the books I write for children. This is a varied level itself, because some of my books, such as *The*

Adventures of Egbert the Easter Egg and *Animals on the Ceiling*, are for first graders, while others, such as *A Dozen Dinosaurs* and *Sea Full of Whales*, are for third or fourth graders and on up—even to adults. Of my other writings, my syndicated weekly light verse feature in *Family Weekly* is for the relatively unsophisticated reader who likes home and family themes. But books such as *It All Started with Stones and Clubs* (collateral reading at West Point) and *The Academic Bestiary* are for advanced and discerning readers. And my verse pieces in *The Wall Street Journal*, now over 2,000 of them, are for those who want some lightness amidst news of the corporations, the government, and the stock market. I'm afraid there are no hidden messages in my work. For the most part, it's shallow, I'll admit. What's there is right on the surface.

JE: Can humor be accurately described as a vehicle for escapism?

RA: Humor isn't escapism for me. I sit by my typewriter every possible hour, seven days a week—and there is no escaping if I wish to keep up my volume of writing. But it may be escapism for my readers, who turn to humor to escape the bad news of the day.

JE: Does humor have lasting literary value? Will it be remembered?

RA: If humor is memorable, it will be remembered. To go beyond this statement of the obvious, I would say that if humor is the sort that is not local, but universal, in its appeal, if it is an original statement of truth, if it uses words well and perhaps in an unusual way, it can have literary value. Perhaps its value is somewhat less than that of serious literature, but Shakespeare's comedies are only a little behind his tragedies. I must admit, however, that *Hamlet*, *King Lear*, *Othello*, and the others have a power greater than that of the comedies. And yet one must not overlook the humor in the tragedies, the comic relief without which the tragedies might be too heavy to bear. Also, there is literary effectiveness in bringing comedy and tragedy together and alternating them not only for relief but for contrast. Or consider the humorous and the serious, comedy and tragedy, as two sides of the coin or two parts of totality. The movies of Charlie Chaplin are a good example of the blend of the comic and the sad. Laugh, clown, laugh. There is something deeply moving about a character in a play or a novel who forces laughter in the midst of desperation.

JE: Is the key to humor more in good writing or in good perception?

RA: Good writing and good perception are about equal in writing humor that will be widely read and will last. I might give the edge to good writing, since good writing can turn an unpromising perception into humor of high quality. Again, I must say that the choice of words, important in all writing, is especially important in writing humor.

JE: How necessary is open-mindedness in writing humor?

RA: Open-mindedness applies more to satire than to humor, unless by open-mindedness you mean having a hole in your head. It is difficult for a satirist to be open-minded, since he is probably writing to improve something, to right a wrong. He will offend those who do not have the same point of view. I may be an exception, but, instead of being open-minded, I may simply be weak. Or I may wish to keep my hold on as many readers as possible.

JE: How do you go about striking a universal chord in your humor?

RA: Sometimes what is universal is not on the surface. It takes some digging, some probing, to discover what is universal or almost universal. I want a broad readership. For several years, I have been asked by lawyers, even the American Bar Association, to write a light, playful, but factual history of law in the style of my many *It All Started with* books. I have come close to doing it, but keep wondering whether there would be enough readers. It is still a possibility, because there are many thousands of lawyers and even more thousands of those who are clients of lawyers. Maybe, maybe.

JE: Are there any major fields you have not tapped in your writing?

RA: Before I wrote *It All Started with Nudes*, my playful history of art (but one that made me read fourteen histories of art and many books on individual artists or schools of art), I had to decide between a history of art and a history of music. I decided on art, partly because I know a little about art but nothing about music, and partly because Campbell Grant, who has illustrated fourteen of my books, teaches history of art. Music is still a possibility. I have thought of doing a history of marriage, though I have done something with it in prose in *My Life with Women* and in verse in *The Spouse in the House*. In fact, I have written a couple of chapters of such a book on this subject. I have also written about fifty pages of a Swiftian work, *How to Eliminate the Human Race*, and may go back to it. However, thinking I couldn't carry it through to book length, I sold the best part of it to *Playboy*, which ran it as an article. Or some hitherto hidden idea may surface. It will have to be a good one.

JE: Does writing humor serve a cathartic value—that is, does it teach you valuable things about yourself?

RA: Yes, writing humor teaches me much about myself. This is especially true in the personal, home-and-family verse feature I write for *Family Weekly*. In fact, it is true of my light verse generally, as collected in *Light Armour, Nights with Armour, An Armoury of Light Verse*, etc. I have published more than 6,000 pieces of light verse in magazines in the United States and England, and the great majority of them are about my everyday experiences. I should know myself by now.

JE: If you were asked to evaluate your work, how would you do so?

RA: I am a minor writer, known more for my light verse than for my prose books of humor. My light verse keeps turning up in anthologies. Several pieces have been set to music, and one is carved on charm bracelets. Another, a quatrain called "Library," is carved in stone in the atrium of a public library. But except for *Light Armour*, now in paperback, my books of prose humor have sold far better than my books of light verse. Also, my prose books have been translated into many languages, including Japanese, but my light verse would be hard to translate. Some know me only for my verses in *The Wall Street Journal*. Others know me only for this or that book or piece of light verse. Sometimes, something of mine is attributed to Ogden Nash. Sometimes, it is attributed to that great writer, "Anon." All of this indicates that I am not exactly a household word. I am grateful for all the recognition I get. I know I have some followers, a few who specialize in collecting my books. These, of course, are the highly literate, discriminating few. Very few.

JE: How do you view your own contribution to the field of humor?

RA: Aside from the light verse, I suppose what I have contributed most to the field of humor is a style of parody of scholarly works, with much word play and many footnotes, the footnotes topping some bit of humor. Some probably think I derived my style, if you can call it that, from Will Cuppy's *The Decline and Fall of Practically Everybody* or Sellar and Yeatman's *1066 And All That*. But though I had read these books earlier, I purposely did not read them again before starting on *It All Started with Columbus*, which, however, I dedicated to Sellar and Yeatman. I think I developed a style of parody of my own, and I kept changing it and I hope improving it with each of the *It All Started with* books. By the time I got to *It All Started with Stones and Clubs*, my satire on the history of war and weaponry, there was little similarity with the style of *It All Started with Columbus*. Maybe there is a little I can call my own.

JE: Do you perceive any new directions in your work?

RA: I continue to write light verse, in the traditional style but perhaps with some Nashian touches, and I write articles on many subjects and in many styles. If my work has taken any new direction, it is to increase the proportion of prose to verse and of satire to humor. But the general direction is still much the same, with the purpose of both entertaining and instructing.

JE: Finally, what projects do you presently have on the drawing board?

RA: At the moment, in addition to *Strange Monsters of the Sea*, now being illustrated by Paul Galdone, I think his tenth with me, I have two books with my literary agent in New York. Both are prose, and one is straight humor, while the other is light-serious. To show how much waiting a writer must endure, whether or not he is a writer of humor, I might mention that one publisher has held one of these books for a full year without reaching a decision. If one of these books is taken by a publisher, I shall probably be in for a period of revision—cutting, adding, rewriting. This is something I find easy in comparison with getting an idea and developing it to book length. And, of course, I must keep the humor or satire at just the right level from beginning to end, using various techniques to hold my reader.

Robert Anton Wilson

Robert Anton Wilson: Searching For Cosmic Intelligence

"The great beasts that inhabited Europe, Asia and North America die off as a result of mutations and diseases caused by the solar flare. All relics of the Atlantean civilization are destroyed. The people who were Gruad's erstwhile countrymen are either killed or driven forth to wander the earth. Besides Gruad's Himalayan colony there is one other remnant of the High Atlantean era; the Pyramid of the Eye, whose ceramic substance resisted solar flare, earthquake, tidal wave and submersion in the depth of the ocean. Gruad explains that it is the right that the eye should remain. It is the eye of God, the One, the scientific-technical eye of ordered knowledge that looks down on the universe and by perceiving it causes it to be. If an event is not witnessed, it does not happen; therefore, for the universe to happen there must be a Witness."

—Robert Shea
Robert Anton Wilson

High atop a hill overlooking the University of California, Berkeley campus, lies the rustic communal retreat of Robert Anton Wilson, the author of over 2,000 articles and nine books, including *Illuminatus!*, the much-acclaimed epic science-fiction satire (written with Robert Shea). A former editor of *Playboy* magazine, Wilson has spent much of his life writing and lecturing on the challenges and opportunities of man's future. In addition, he is the president of the Exo-Psychology Institute in Berkeley and a director of the Prometheus Society, as well as a charter member and advocate of Gerard O'Neill's proposals for space colonization. His most recent work, *Cosmic Trigger: The Final Secret of the Illuminati*, is the nonfiction sequel to his novels on the subject. *Illuminatus!* represents a synthesis of new trends in physics and parapsychology, combining elements of science fiction and political satire, and revolving around such contemporary interests as UFOs, holistic health, cosmology, quantum mechanics, and human consciousness. Several critics believe it is destined to become the most popular science fiction cult novel since Frank Herbert's *Dune*.

Robert Anton Wilson is an important thinker and doer, a renowned mystic and revolutionary whose books and articles are read and debated with gusto and fervor. His work has won the plaudits of the literary establishment as well as the literary underground. Alan Watts has dubbed his writing as "subversive, esoteric, and extremely interesting." Tim Leary has acclaimed it "scholarly, literate, witty, and great!" David Harris has proclaimed it "the anarchist acid-rock answer to Tolkien." Henry Miller has declared it "something we've needed for a long time!"

When I arrived for the interview, Wilson was smiling and accomodating. He led me into his front room, which was chockfull of books and papers. After chatting a while, and discussing the merits of freshly squeezed orange juice, we began our dialogue. An incisive and entertaining conversationalist, Wilson was animated and engrossing. He talked for nearly five hours—without a let-up—exploring such provocative topics as space colonization, libertarianism, life extension, Tim Leary, Magick, higher intelligence, the Illuminati, and Guerilla Ontology, among others.

There is something quite inexplicable about Bob Wilson—perhaps it is his earthy wisdom or his mystical propensities. In this regard, the author holds titles as an initiate in several occult orders, including White Cord Witch, Voodoo Priest, Water Broker, and High Priest of the Cult of the Sacred Cyborg. Whatever the key is to the Wilson persona, I came away from the interview buoyed and optimistic. His energy and vitality proved intoxicating. I left feeling that I had, yes, made contact with the higher intelligence! In the interview that follows, Wilson discusses a wide range of subjects, constantly striving to forge a workable synthesis of both the scientific and mystical traditions. In the end, what emerges is a striking discourse on the nature of reality—what it is and what it isn't—and why such a synthesis is vital to our planet's future.

*   *   *   *   *

JE: What made you want to be a writer?

RAW: As far back as I can remember, I wanted to be a storyteller. When I was twelve years old, I started drawing comic strips, which I circulated among other kids in the neighborhood. When I was fourteen years old, I discovered there were books made up of nothing but words. It seemed much easier to just write the words rather than having to do the drawings to accompany them. I wrote my first novel that year and, of course, I couldn't get it published. It was about a meek mild reporter, somewhat like Clark Kent, who drank a potion which turned him into a virtual Superman-type character. His name was Danny Dingle, because it was a comedy rather than a melodrama. In my youthful naivete, I thought I could sell it as a movie starring Danny Kate. I wrote quite a few short stories in my teens, all of which were rejected. As a result, I decided to become an engineer and write in the evenings. I knew I needed a money-making occupation until I became a success as a writer. Well, after five years as an engineering aide, I realized I couldn't be a writer and an engineer at the same time. It was too demanding in terms of time, so I decided to become, instead, an English teacher. Along the way, I got married and ended up in the advertising business instead of teaching English. I spent about three years in advertising and then escaped, thank God, relatively undamaged. I've spent most of my life since then in various editorial positions at a number of publications. It took me an awfully long time to get my first book into print. In fact, I sold over 2,000 articles to various magazines before landing my first book sale. I suppose I have more articles in print than any other living writer.

JE: At what point in this process did you know you could make it as a full-time writer without having to take a second job in order to supplement your income?

RAW: I've only been able to support myself as a full-time writer in the last three years.

JE: What kinds of jobs did you take along the way while you were trying to establish yourself as a professional writer?

RAW: As I mentioned, I worked in numerous editorial jobs. I was also a medical orderly, a salesman, a longshoreman, and an executive. In addition, I was an associate editor of *Playboy* for nearly six years. Also, I worked for a sweat shop in New York, where I edited five magazines simultaneously. Actually, this meant I wrote practically everything in the magazines under a variety of pen names. They had a very low budget. I got $125 a week before taxes for editing the five publications. I had a lot of other jobs like that. I was an editor of Ralph Ginsberg's *Fact* magazine for a while (which is what Ginsberg did after *Eros* was suppressed by the Supreme Court, and before he started *Moneysworth* magazine).

JE: What formal training did you have as a writer?

RAW: I took one course in writing at New York University.

JE: Have you ever found your lack of formal training a handicap in developing an effective writing style?

RAW: No. The first piece of writing I submitted in that writing class caused the teacher to remark that it was the most professional piece of writing she had ever seen and that I should be a full-time writer, which simply confirmed my own opinion. So, really, I developed my style on my own.

JE: Can you see in your own writing style specific influences in terms of other writers whose work you admire?

RAW: Oh, very definitely. I can easily look at my own prose and see whose voices are represented. There's a great deal of Ezra Pound, a great deal of James Joyce, a great deal of Raymond Chandler, a touch of Norman Mailer, and a soupcon of H. L. Mencken.

JE: Did any of these writers prove helpful in the sense of teaching you about the process of writing itself?

RAW: Yes. For example, from Pound I learned that every sentence should have a life of its own. There should be no empty sentences. Basically, there are two types of writers: one type is interested in getting the damned thing done and sold, while the second type really enjoy writing and want every sentence to have its own wit, its own beauty. Pound converted me into the second type of writer. I want every sentence to contain a bit of pleasure for me and for the attentive reader. From Mailer, I learned how to write long sentences that are modern and swing. Faulkner writes long sentences, but one gets lost in the syntax; one doesn't get lost in Mailer. Joyce taught me a great deal about how to vary the tone of a paragraph and create emotional effects that are almost subliminal, and how to convey very subtle psychological processes. Chandler was a major influence, in the sense that there's not a single dull sentence in any of his books. I've tried to follow that practice in my own writing. It's odd, but I can't think of a single science-fiction writer who has significantly influenced my style of writing. What I have learned from science-fiction writers, though, is to have an open attitude towards the future. In this sense, they've influenced my philosophy more than my style.

JE: What is it about writing that fascinates you?

RAW: Well, I think it's a kind of hedonic-controlled schizophrenia. It's also a kind of yoga, especially novel-writing. Full-time writing is a constant daily exercise in getting outside one's own head and thinking and feeling the way other people think and feel. I often think of it in terms of Gurdjieff's work. Gurdjieff, the Russian mystic, devoted most of his energy to teaching his pupils how to get outside their own egos and see the world the way other people see it. I've become very interested in his work in the last four or five years, and it has occured to me that what he is teaching is what every good novelist learns if he sticks with being a writer. One can't create characters who are simply variations of oneself. One must go way out and create characters who are nothing like oneself. When one does that, one really learns something about humanity. In that sense, I think novel writing is more educational for the novelist than for the reader.

JE: Is writing more an innate need to express yourself or something you do simply to support yourself?

RAW: It's sheer pleasure. As I said before, I'm definitely a style-oriented writer. Every paragraph is a challenge, and when I get the paragraph organized just the right way, I experience a great sense of bliss, such as a mathematician experiences when he solves a difficult equation. It's a head game, a brain exercise, and it's lots of fun if one's attuned to that type of mental exercise. Every writing project is a growth project, especially if one has the aim, as I have, of never repeating myself. I keep trying to do things I've never done before, which means that every writing job entails another brain-change operation.

JE: Do you write with a particular audience in mind? Does audience figure into what you write and how you write it?

RAW: Obviously, not as much as it should or I would have been more successful much sooner. Insofar as I have any audience in mind, it's not the audience I should have in mind. I tend to write for the most hip and intelligent people I can envision, which is not necessarily the way to commercial success. I must constantly remind myself that there are other audiences, too, and I must try to please them as well. Unfortunately, I always tend to slip back into writing for an elite audience. However, I try to put things into my books that appeal to a larger audience. For example, *Illuminatus!* has enough sex and violence in it to satisfy any television fan.

JE: How, then, would you describe your audience?

RAW: Actually, I have several audiences. My work appeals to those who are interested in Kabala, ceremonial magic, and occultism. There are political libertarians who dig my work because of the anti-government satire. Scientists and science-fiction fans also enjoy my work because of my comic use of ideas from modern physics.

JE: Is a book fully organized in your mind before you start writing, or does it take shape as it develops?

RAW: Sometimes, I have a clearer idea of where I'm going than other times, but it always surprises me. In the course of writing, I'm always drawing on my unconscious creativity, and I find things creeping into my writing that I wasn't aware of at the time. That's part of the pleasure of writing. After you've written something, you say to yourself, "Where in the hell did that come from?" Faulkner called it the "demon" that directs the writer. The Kabalists call it the "holy guardian angel." Every writer experiences this sensation. Robert E. Howard said he felt there was somebody dictating the Conan stories to him. There's some deep level of the unconscious that knows a lot more than the conscious mind of the writer knows.

JE: How meticulous a writer are you? Do you agonize over the language and structure?

RAW: I'm very meticulous, but I don't agonize. It's all a lot of fun, and no more "agonizing" than anyone else's favorite hobby. It varies, however, according to what I'm writing. I've written some things as many as sixteen times before I was satisfied with the finished product, but I enjoy myself the whole time. Sometimes, I enjoy myself so much that I collapse from exhaustion. I've been known to work from sixteen to twenty hours and collapse with a very stiff back and wake up the next morning with an acute case of conjunctivitis. Even there, I enjoyed myself all the way through it.

JE: When you write, do you follow a set regimen?

RAW: Yes, in a rough sort of way. I start some time in the morning, usually around nine to eleven o'clock, depending on my mood or how much I want to sit around over breakfast talking to my family. Generally, I try to knock off between five and six o'clock. Frequently, though, I get a second burst after dinner and go back and write for several more hours. However, that doesn't happen too often any more. It happened more when I was broke, desperate, and struggling to turn out as much material as I could in order to make ends meet.

JE: Does writing serve a therapeutic value for you? Have you learned important things about yourself as a result of writing?

RAW: Oh yes, definitely. I would say, though, I've gotten more surprises out of LSD than I've gotten out of writing.

JE: Are you an admirer of your own work? Do you generally like what you've written?

RAW: Yes, very much so. I tend to be childishly delighted with everything I write. Every now and then, though, I'm very unhappy with a certain piece and can't bring myself to submit it anywhere. Usually, in a case like that, after about three months, I'll take it out, rewrite it, and submit it elsewhere.

JE: Is writing a natural act for you? Does it come easily to you?

RAW: Oh, yes. It comes as easily to me as tennis comes to a professional tennis player. It's my game. To me, it's the third best thing in the world, after sex and Chinese food.

JE: Are you affected by the critics? Do their opinions concern you?

RAW: As William Butler Yeats said, "Was there ever a dog that loved its fleas?" Critics have been very kind to me, personally. Of all the reviews of my published books, something like 90 percent have been highly favorable, so I have no personal grudge against critics. On the other hand, in an impersonal way, I have a strong moral objection to critics. Whenever I see a critic tearing a writer or actor or any artist to shreds in print, I feel a sense of revulsion. I write a lot of criticism myself, but I only review things I like. I don't admire the desire to tear other people apart. I can only think of two unfavorable reviews I've written in my whole life, and I regret them. One was about a book in which a woman gets raped and is said to enjoy it; the other was a review of a very dogmatic book about UFOs, in which the author described those who disagreed with him as neurotics. People who like to write witty, nasty things about other people are not generous or charitable, to put it mildly. We should all try to give out as much good energy to other human beings as we possibly can. I honestly believe that every bit of bad energy we put out has adverse effects that go on forever. This is the Buddhist doctrine of karma. The Buddhists believe that every bit of anger, resentment, hate and so on that goes out passes from one person to another, without stopping. The same is true of good energy: every bit of good energy one puts out makes someone else feel a little bit better. I think if people were really conscious of this psychological fact, they would try very, very hard to put out nothing but good energy, no matter what happened to them. They would certainly not be so casual about passing on bad energy. All the bad energy in the world builds up like a giant snowfall, until we have a huge war. Nowadays, it can mean a total nuclear Armageddon. This is traditional Buddhism, as I say, but I think it's materialistic common sense, too. One only needs to study human behavior to realize it. I regard those people who make a career out of being nasty as emotional plague carriers.

JE: As you review some of the pieces you wrote early in your career, can you see signs of major stylistic improvement?

RAW: I hope so. I would rather be gored by a rhinoceros than see some of my 1950s pieces be reprinted now! Even some of my 1960s pieces, I hope, are lost forever.

JE: In what ways has your writing improved over the years?

RAW: I hope I'm less acerbic, less dogmatic, less moralistic, and more charitable.

JE: Are you concerned that your work have didactic value, that people learn from it?

RAW: Absolutely! Didactic literature is very much out of style these days; if one is suspected of having a message, it's almost regarded as some kind of impurity. I think, however, that all first-rate literature is didactic. Dante is didactic. Shakespeare is didactic. Melville is didactic. Science fiction is the most didactic literature around; that's why I enjoy it so much. All writers are teachers, whether they're conscious of it or not, or whether they'll admit it or not. For example, take Mickey Spillane. He used to give interviews in which he said he only wrote books for money. However, if you look at his work, it's obvious he has very strong beliefs. He's always pitching them at the reader. They're rather fascist beliefs, but they're beliefs, nonetheless, and he's a teacher, just like every other writer. Unfortunately, he's only teaching a violent, fascist morality.

JE: You seem to be a virtual storehouse of ideas. Do you file ideas away, keep a notebook, or record your thoughts?

RAW: When I'm working on a novel, I keep notes on things that occur to me that can't be used in that particular work. I might use these thoughts at a later time, which is why I go through the effort of recording them. By and large, I don't keep notebooks, except one special notebook, in which I record dreams, synchronisticies, and occult happenings. I like to have a record of such things, just so I can check it every so often and see if there are any significant patterns emerging.

JE: Are you still an active reader? Does being a writer afford you much time for reading?

RAW: No. That's one of the paradoxes of a writer's life: the more successful one becomes, the less time one has to read. I spend so much time writing that, generally, by the time I knock off for the day, my eyes are too tired to do much reading. I used to read a book a day when I was younger. Now, if I manage a book a week, it's unusual. A book every two weeks is more common for me now.

JE: Your writing is said to be very symbolic in content. Do you pre-plan your use of symbolism or does it creep in by accident?

RAW: Oh, I'm very tricky that way. My books are full of hidden gimmicks— not just symbols, but very obscure jokes, cross-references, and parodies of other writers. I feel I'm giving future Ph.Ds a vast field for research.

JE: You're a writer who's known for having an enormous cult following. What explains this underground interest in your work?

RAW: Actually, I have several cult followings, not just one. That's amusing. I've got fans who like me for one reason, others who like me for another reason, and neither are aware of the other. I have no idea why my work generates this interest, but I would like to think it's because I'm a very funny writer. Of course, there's the fact that an awful lot of my writing comes out of very deep levels of the unconscious. I incorporate into my writing a lot of stuff from my dreams and from various yogic and magickal exercises that turn on parts of the brain that connect with what Jung calls "the archetypes of collective unconscious." So, there's probably a level in my work that's mythic, in the sense that *King Kong* is mythic or *Lord of the Rings* is mythic. I don't know if it's that archetypal level that explains the interest in my work, or whether it's just the humor. Perhaps it's a mixture of the two.

JE: Are you ever amused when you hear people discuss the symbolic significance of some passage in your work, when you know full-well it has no symbolic significance whatsoever?

RAW: No. Everything in my writing operates on several levels at once. Any symbolism people find in my work was probably intended to be there, especially since I employ so much dream material.

JE: If one were to examine the more than 2,000 articles you've authored, could one discern any salient themes or ideas which seem to repeat themselves over and over again?

RAW: Yes. From the beginning, my writing has had a clear libertarian bias. It has always contained a good deal of anti-government propaganda. Moreover, there has always been an element of self-mockery in my writing, because I feel uncomfortable being on a pedestal, and so I try to encourage the reader not to take me too seriously. Furthermore, I've always written on a variety of topics, for a variety of audiences. I've never limited myself to any one field or area.

JE: Can you say something about the genesis of *Illuminatus!*? How did the idea unfold in your mind?

RAW: It started with the Discordian Society, which is based on worship of Eris, the Greek goddess of confusion and chaos. Actually, the Discordian Society is a new religion disguised as a complicated joke, although some skeptics think it's a joke disguised as a religion. We (Bob Shea, his co-author) felt the Society needed some opposition, because the whole idea of it is based on conflict and dialectics. So, we created an opposition within the Discordian Society, which we called the Bavarian Illuminati. We got the idea from the John Birch Society and various other right-wing groups who believe that the Illuminati really run the world. There were several Discordian newsletters written in the 1960s, and several Discordian members wrote for the underground press in various parts of the country. So, we built up this myth about the warfare between the Discordian Society and the Illuminati for quite a while, until one day Bob Shea said to me, "You know, we could write a novel about this!" The rest is history.

JE: When you began the project, did you ever envision that it would take on such massive proportions, both in terms of scope and direction?

RAW: No. When we started, Bob and I planned to write a fairly short novel. Once we got into it, though, we got carried away and it got longer and longer. Bob kept telling me, "It's getting too long," and I kept saying, "Yeah, but this is good stuff, isn't it?" Eventually, the book was so long that when Dell finally accepted it, they insisted that we cut 500 pages.

JE: In what sense is the book science fact as opposed to science fiction?

RAW: I wanted to write a book that combined several different literary genres. As a result, *Illuminatus!* is a combination detective story, occult thriller, political satire, and science-fiction work, with overtones of a porno novel, a dissertation on politics, and an occult fantasy. It constantly keeps changing. Whenever the reader thinks he knows where it's going, it turns into another type of novel. That was part of our problem in selling it. Publishers don't like that; they like a novel they can easily label. I'm still struggling with this problem in my present writing. My next book, *Masks of the Illuminati*, is something the publisher is going to have a hard time finding a label for, because it deliberately starts out as one type of novel and turns into an entirely different type of novel. This, to me, is realism. After all, life doesn't fall into categories. People don't live their whole lives in detective stories or gothic thrillers or soap operas or science-fiction novels or Hitchcock dramas. People's lives change from day to day, from hour to hour. I've always wanted to write novels in which the reader doesn't know what kind of script he's living in. Publishers can't stand this approach. They want to put a label on a story, and I keep trying to break that restriction. This is all part of my insidious campaign to undermine the minds of readers who think they know what they're reading. I want people to realize that literature isn't always what they think it is. Then they might realize that life isn't what they think it is.

JE: One label that has been applied to your work by you yourself is "anarchist fiction." In what sense can your writing be described by this label?

RAW: My early work is politically anarchist fiction, in that I was an anarchist for a long period of time. I'm not an anarchist any longer, because I've concluded that anarchism is an impractical ideal. Nowadays, I regard myself as a libertarian. I suppose an anarchist would say, paraphrasing what Marx said about agnostics being "frightened atheists," that libertarians are simply frightened anarchists. Having just stated the case for the opposition, I will go along and agree with them: yes, I am frightened. I'm a libertarian because I don't trust the people as much as anarchists do. I want to see government limited as much as possible; I would like to see it reduced back to where it was in Jefferson's time, or even smaller. But I would not like to see it abolished. I think the average American, if left totally free, would act exactly like Idi Amin. I don't trust the people any more than I trust the government.

JE: Many people think that *Illuminatus!* can also be viewed as "anarchist fiction" in the sense that it employs a multitude of writing styles and techniques. Would you agree with their assessment?

RAW: Yes. However, I didn't invent that method. Joyce did the same thing in *Ulysses*. Every chapter of *Ulysses* is written in a different style. I don't think *Illuminatus!* is quite as original as a lot of people who only read science fiction think it is. The basic structure which has aroused so much controversy is boldly lifted from D. W. Griffith's movie *Intolerance*. I think *Intolerance* is the greatest movie ever made, so I stole everything I could find from it. I'm very much in love with Griffith's technique of montage. *Illuminatus!* is written just the way Griffith edited his films. In *Intolerance*, he has four stories set in four different periods of history. He continuously goes back and forth between the four. That's basically the technique I used in *Illuminatus!* It's amusing to me that people find it so startling when it was done in film as early as 1915, when *Intolerance* was made.

JE: How do you respond to the charge that the book lacks a sense of thematic unity, that it strays from idea to idea without ever resolving any of the ideas themselves?

RAW: The same kind of criticism could be leveled against *Don Quixote, Moby Dick*, and *Ulysses*, which are three of my favorite novels. I'm writing for an audience that digs that type of artistic encyclopedia. Those readers whose attention span is much shorter should ignore *Illuminatus!* and stick to "Little Orphan Annie."

JE: You've characterized your own writing as "guerrilla ontology." What does that term imply?

RAW: The western world has been brainwashed by Aristotle for the last 2,500 years. The unconscious, not quite articulate relief of most occidentals is that there is one map which adequately represents reality. By sheer good luck, every occidental thinks he or she has the map that fits. Guerilla ontology, to me, involves shaking up that certainty. I use what in modern physics is called the "multi-model approach," which is the idea that there is more than one model to cover a given set of facts. As I've said, novel writing involves learning to think like other people. My novels are written so as to force the reader to see things through different reality grids rather than through a single grid. It's important to abolish the unconscious dogmatism that makes people think their way of looking at reality is the only sane way of viewing the world. My goal is to try to get people into a state of generalized agnosticism, not agnosticism about God alone, but agnosticism about everything. If one can only see things according to one's own belief system, one is destined to become virtually deaf, dumb, and blind. It's only possible to see people when one is able to see the world as others see it. That's what guerilla ontology is—breaking down this one-model view and giving people a multi-model view.

JE: For those who have not read *Illuminatus!* and would like to know something about the storyline of the book, how would you describe its overall thrust and purpose?

RAW: I like the description by John White, in his review of the book, who said, "It's a journey through paranoia to metanoia." Paranoia is a state of mind in which one is able to see that everything is connected, which indeed it is, but the paranoid sees everything connected in the form of a conspiracy directed at him. In metanoia, you see that everything is connected, but in a very funny, comical, and ultimately triumphant way. I would say that the end of Beethoven's *Ninth Symphony* is the greatest expression of metanoia in western art. Every successful mystic has a basically metanoid outlook on life. Anyone who has ever taken LSD has experienced a few hours of metanoia.

JE: How do we get people to move away from the view that there is a single answer to a given problem?

RAW: Well, that started breaking down with the rise of urban civilization and commerce. As long as people lived in tribes, it was very easy to think that "our way of looking at things was the only correct way." When piracy and nomadic raiding parties developed, people could still think that way. However, when people started trading and having commerce with one another, they had to learn to see things the way other people saw them. As a result, some sense of cultural relativism appeared in the ancient Greeks, who were great traders. I think that's what's responsible for the rise in Greek philosophy. Unfortunately, this has always remained a minority point of view because of the entrenched power of dogmatic thought. With the rise of modern electronics and technology, however, things have begun to change faster. We're now living in the global village which Buckminster Fuller and Marshal McLuhan have long been predicting. I've actually met people in their twenties who have travelled to as many as thirty different countries in their lives. With that amount of travel and the emergence of modern electronic media, more and more people are developing a sense of cultural relativism. This leads directly to what I call "neurological relativism," which is the recognition that the way one's nervous system organizes impressions into Gestalts is not the only possible way; and that everyone else's nervous system is likewise organizing an entirely different reality. They're all equally real because they're all an outgrowth of human experience.

JE: *Illuminatus!* is a collaborative effort, written with the assistance of Bob Shea. Did you enjoy the process of collaboration? Did it pose any special problems?

RAW: Actually, I've done a number of collaborations, as well as six books on my own. I wrote *Illuminatus!* with Shea and I wrote *Neuropolitics* with Tim Leary, as well as another book with Leary which hasn't been published yet, entitled *The Neurological Tarot.* I find that writing alone and collaborating are both fun in different ways. The collaborations worked very well with both Shea and Leary. I would be delighted to collaborate with either of them in the future. I suppose there are some people who, if I tried to collaborate with them, would drive me to going up the wall or chewing up the carpet. I think one has to choose one's collaborators quite carefully.

JE: How do you explain the fact that while you've produced so much work, and really excellent work, you've yet to really crack the literary mainstream?

RAW: I think the answer is genetic. If one studies the evolution of gene pools, it's clear that humanity began somewhere in the east and has been migrating steadily westward. I think it's the more adventuresome, far out, exploratory genes which have travelled west. Most of my fan mail comes from the west coast—California, Washington, Oregon, and Arizona. The official intelligentsia of the United States, by which I mean those who have declared themselves to be the intelligentsia, all live in New York. Genetically, they're a separate stock from the westerner. Westerners are a totally different breed of people, and I don't think it's any accident that Tom Robbins, Thomas Pynchon, Ted Sturgeon, Tim Leary, and I all live in the west. To the eastern intelligentsia, the latest things in science are Marx and Freud; they simply haven't heard of anything since then. There's an entirely different genetic stock and neurological set in the east. Basically, I would say they're about seventy years behind in terms of neurological evolution.

JE: In what sense is *Illuminatus!* a product of your own experiences with drugs, such as LSD?

RAW: I suppose it's a product of my drug experiences, but it's also a product of my experiences of being tear-gassed by the Chicago cops, my experiences of being an editor at *Playboy*, my experiences of being a welfare recipient, and my experiences of going up and down and down and up the economic ladder.

JE: Let's talk about the issue of space colonization. There are many people who view this as such a remote possibility that they find it difficult to take the whole idea seriously. Do you see space colonization as a real possibility within the foreseeable future?

RAW: Yes. I think space habitats are absolutely inevitable in the next thirty years. The only remaining question is, how soon? All of the major problems confronting this planet will either be alleviated or solved once we start building space colonies. By 2025, there will be more people leaving this planet than being born on it, so that the population will simply wither away. I think solar power derived from space is the first step toward creating worldwide affluence and abolishing poverty and starvation. Space is also a great hope in terms of enlarging human freedom, because freedom is always found on the perimeter of society, on the expanding wave. Freedom is the vector of where the pioneers went, to get as far away as possible from the nearest government. The art of freedom is to keep moving on the expanding wave. That's why all the most libertarian people are piled up on this side of the Rockies or in Hawaii. The industrial frontier is closed, so the next place for the libertarian to go is into space. As Tim Leary likes to say, "In space, the lesbian vegetarians can have their own habitat in fifty years." Everybody who wants to create a new type of society will have a chance to join forces with like-minded individuals and create their own utopia. That happened in this country in the nineteenth century. There were over 1,000 "intentional communities," as sociologists call them, that were utopian in nature and founded on the frontier. Some of them failed, some of them partially succeeded, and some of them were eventually incorporated by the federal government as it expanded its powers. A few still survive today, although under the control of the federal government, like the Amish community. Basically, the argument for space is that we need the energy and that it's a chance for societal experiments which are impossible on this planet under present conditions of increasingly omnipotent governments.

JE: Do you sense a growing national commitment to space colonization?

RAW: Yes. Very much so. A number of studies have been done which confirm that the majority of kids in grammar school expect to go into space by the time they grow up, and I think they're quite right in expecting that to happen. More people have been in space now than had flown the Atlantic fifty years ago. If you use aeronautics as your model, taking the years 1928 to 1978, you will find that one person flew the Atlantic in 1928, while 200 million people did so in 1978. Projecting space forward at the same rate, there's likely to be more than 200 million people leaving Earth in 2028. Moreover, for anybody with good old American cupidity in their heart, the quickest way to become a millionaire is to invest in space technology, space industry, and so on. There's an awful lot of raw materials out there. It represents the greatest real estate boom we've ever experienced.

JE: How does this square with the present lack of federal resolve in this area?

RAW: The government's foot-dragging suits me fine. I would much rather see space opened to settlement by private industry than by government. I don't think that space colonization should become a government monopoly. Sadly, the government is only interested in space from the military angle, and that has turned out to be not as significant as they thought. Moreover, government in this country is made up chiefly of lawyers, and lawyers are always oriented toward the past. What does a lawyer do when preparing a case? He looks for precedents; in other words, he looks up the past. I think if our Congress were made up largely of engineers, or if we had as many engineers in Congress as we have lawyers, Congress would be much more oriented to the future and the space program would be rocketing ahead at incredible speed.

JE: You've written a good deal in recent years about UFOs. From your perspective, how do you evaluate the myriad claims that have been made for their existence?

RAW: As usual, I would approach this question from a multi-model perspective. I think these UFOs may be extra-terrestrials; but, I also think they may be a lot of other things. They may be extra-dimensional, rather than extraterrestrial; they may also be time travellers from the future. One of my favorite theories is that UFOs are created by their witnesses. I think it's quite likely that psychokinesis exists, and just as some disturbed adolescents create "ghosts," others work themselves into an excited state of mind in which they project UFOs. I think it's very likely that UFOs are created by the human mind to fill a need that humanity feels at this point in history; it may be a precognitive signal of our own extra-terrestrial future. However, I don't insist on the validity of any one of these theories. It could be any one of these things or a combination of all of them or some category that we haven't yet invented.

JE: The charge has often been made that the government has willfully and deliberately withheld information relating to the existence of UFOs. Do you share that view?

RAW: Oh, I believe the government willfully and deliberately withholds information every chance it can. Basically, the government doesn't trust the people—which reminds me of Bertold Brecht's immortal remark: "If the government doesn't trust the people, why doesn't the government dissolve them and elect a new people?" The government hides everything, whether they have a reason for hiding it or not; it's simply a reflex action. Information to a governing body is a weapon. Governments specialize in withholding information and also in spreading false information, for exactly the same reason that poker players do. It's an excellent strategy to win a competitive advantage.

JE: How do you respond to the charge that spending increased revenues on space and space colonization rechannels those same funds away from badly needed domestic programs?

RAW: In the first place, I think space colonization should be carried out by private industry rather than by government, so that argument doesn't really apply. In the second place, I think people who raise that objection don't fully understand how much we've already benefitted from space exploration. It's absolutely staggering when one considers the number of technological advances that have come out of NASA and been applied here on Earth. For instance, Buckminster Fuller, in his book *I Seem to Be a Verb*, includes a long list of things developed by NASA which have proven to be extremely beneficial on Earth. Moreover, Arthur Clarke has estimated that the improvement in our ability to predict the weather, brought about by the development of weather satellites, has saved the farmers alone so much money that that in itself would support the entire space program.

JE: Do you share the conviction that NASA has done a poor job of selling the space program to the American people, in the sense that it has played up the development of teflon pans as opposed to major medical advantages?

RAW: Yes, I do. I think NASA has an inept and clumsy style as far as public relations go. Hell, after the success of the Moon landing, one of their top officials was quoted as saying, "This is a triumph of the crewcut guys who aren't ashamed to say a prayer now and then," thereby, in one great proclamation, insulting everybody who had long hair, everybody who wasn't male, and everybody who didn't believe in the Judaic-Christian God. That idiot managed to offend three-fourths of the population in one fell swoop, and, of course, what he said wasn't true. NASA was built on the efforts of scientists over the last 3,000 years, including some who had long hair, like Einstein, many who were rabid atheists, like Haekle, some who were female, like Marie Curie, and many others who would emphatically not be regarded as respectable citizens by middle-class America. I think NASA is a masterpiece of stupidity in the field of public relations.

JE: Given the enormous number of by-products which have come from science and scientific exploration, why is it that the average American has so little knowledge of and interest in science, even in its most basic sense?

RAW: I think it's chiefly due to the activities of organized religion. Any teacher who tries to impart a really scientific outlook to students in grammar school, or even in high school, would come in for sharp criticism; to some extent, this is true even at the college level. The teacher who really tried to convey to students the skepticism of the scientific outlook, the ability to distinguish a real argument from a lot of pompous noise, would fare very badly at most institutions. Organized religion, advertising, and politics are all based on perpetuating naivete and stupidity, so none of them are anxious to see people become more intelligent and rational. They wouldn't want to see an educated, intelligent population—they wouldn't know how to manipulate them.

JE: Many of the concerns that run central to your life, such as mysticism, the occult, and magic are often themselves the butt of jokes on the part of large numbers of people. They're frequently dismissed as too bizarre or outlandish to warrant serious examination. Why do people go to such great lengths to discredit that which they don't understand?

RAW: Well, it's a question of hive solidarity. Every mammalian or insect colony is terrified of the mutant of the one who doesn't play his assigned role in the hive or the pack. For example, the German secret police, at one point, were trailing Immanuel Kant around, and his philosophy had nothing to do with politics, really; the fact that he was a rational, thinking human being was enough to frighten them out of their wits. Right now, the occult is the area we're not supposed to think about. It frightens people much the same way.

JE: Another salient idea that looms important in your writing is that of immortality and the entire question of life extension. How did you become interested in this area?

RAW: It came gradually. I heard about cryonics in the late 1960s, and at that time it seemed like a very long shot to me. Then in the early 1970s, I started hearing about various new approaches to life extension. The more I heard about the subject, the more interested I became. I now believe it's very likely that within this generation we will see the first dramatic breakthrough in longevity. I would not want to predict what the first breakthrough would give us in terms of additional years, but assuming that we each had only thirty years more than we presently have, that means most of us would be living on to the point where the more enthusiastic researchers into life extension could conceivably raise our life span to 400 years or more. There are presently a number of scientists, such as Dr. Paul Siegal, who believe we can raise human life to 400 to 800 years. Even if they're a generation premature, I think we're going to see a dramatic jump in life extension in this generation, which means that we'll live on for another generation of researchers. These researchers will very likely achieve what the more optimistic researchers today are aiming at: life spanning the centuries, then the millennia.

JE: Many of your books call upon the reader to view the world from alternative perspectives. As you see it, what are some of the best ways to bring about this mind-expansion?

RAW: I really don't know of any legitimate ways to do it to somebody else. Almost any way you do it to somebody else is disguised brainwashing. The only legitimate one to experiment on is yourself, I think. Of course, if you're a professional therapist and people come to you voluntarily, that's quite a different matter. I don't approve, though, of involuntary commitment to mental hospitals. I think there are many known ways of changing people's heads around—putting them into a different reality—ranging from chemical methods to electro-shock to isolation to the traditional brainwashing techniques used by totalitarian governments. I object to all these methods, unless the person has volunteered to have his brain changed. As far as experimenting on oneself is concerned, I think that's one's constitutional right, and no government has the authority to interfere with it. If people want to alter their consciousness with heroin, for example, they have that right. If they want to try electro-shock, they have that right. If they want to go through scientology, they have that right. Nobody, however, has the right to give them heroin against their will, or electro-shock against their will, or force them into scientology against their will, or force them to take drugs against their will.

JE: For you personally, what kinds of mind-expansion techniques have proved most valuable?

RAW: To be absolutely honest, I can't be sure what techniques have benefitted me the most, mainly because I've tried so many different techniques. I don't know which ones deserve the most credit or blame for where my head is at. With that caveat, I suspect the techniques which have helped me the most have been ones I've learned from Tim Leary and Aleister Crowley. However, I've tried so many different techniques that I can't evaluate their individual effects. For example, I may have derived tangible benefits out of semantics twenty-five years after I stopped studying it. I was in rather orthodox Freudian therapy back in my twenties, and that may have loosened me up to a considerable extent. Maybe that's why I was able to respond more favorably to LSD than many other people who have experimented with its use.

JE: Many people view mind-expanding drugs, such as LSD, as extremely dangerous, both to the individual and to society at large. How would you respond to the charge that the use of drugs, such as LSD, have extremely deleterious consequences, and that the potential benefits are not worth the possible risks?

RAW: As you suggest, LSD is a powerful brain-change agent. As such, it's extremely dangerous to the average American, especially those who don't use it, but just read about it. It creates all sorts of paranoid trips in them. Among those who use it, I've seen some serious damage done. However, I think the benefits are also tremendous, especially when used by professionals who really understand what they're doing. In short, LSD is a potentially beneficial change-agent, but there are very few people capable of using it effectively at the present time. As a result, I discourage its widespread use, especially since most of what's called LSD these days is not LSD at all, but all sorts of things containing varying degrees of speed and other garbage.

JE: Tim Leary has had a profound impact on you, both in terms of your life and work. How would you assess Leary's role as an "educator," and what contributions has he made to the advancement of modern society?

RAW: Leary has made a number of salient contributions. In the first place, the Leary Interpersonal Grid is one of the most widely used diagnostic tools in the nation. In fact, it was used on Leary himself when he first arrived in the California prison system. An understanding of the grid will give you a better appreciation of yourself and other people. Leary's comprehension of LSD, I think, is superior to any other scientist who has written about it; he understands it and knows how to use it constructively. He recognizes, as few others do, that LSD suspends the printed neurological programs of one's life, thereby creating imprint vulnerability, in which a new imprint can be created. This means that if one is working with someone who understands LSD, or the person himself understands it, it is possible to create an entirely new ego for oneself. On the other hand, if one is simply experimenting casually with it, one is likely to imprint anything (including delusions).

JE: A prominent theme that runs throughout your writing is that of libertarianism. How would you like to see the government reshaped, recast, so that it would be more in line with libertarian thought and practice?

RAW: First of all, I would like to see all of the "top secret" and "confidential" stamps thrown in the Potomac. I would like the government to be totally open. A government that hides things from its own people becomes implicitly totalitarian, and, as we have seen in the last twenty years, becomes explicitly totalitarian very rapidly. I don't think government should ever hide things from its citizens. So, if I were asked to reform things, the first thing I would do is pass a law requiring the government to open its activities to scrutiny by any citizen, simply on the basis of being a citizen. Anybody should have the right to walk into any building in Washington and say, "I want to see what's going on here!" and nothing should be hidden from them. If we don't have that, we don't have democracy.

JE: In addition to openness in government, what other areas of American life would you reform?

RAW: I'm all for the taxpayers' revolt which started here among the genetic mutants in California. I would like to see it spread throughout the entire country. I think the ideal government would be supported entirely by voluntary contributions, like any other business contraption. If people think they're getting something useful from government, they'll be glad to pay for it. If not, they won't. I think the government should compete on the free market with Lockheed, General Motors, and the Pinkerton Detective Agency. If one wants protection, one should have the right to choose whether one wants the FBI or the Pinkertons. I don't especially trust the FBI, so if I felt I needed protection, I would personally go to the Pinkertons. I think government should be a free-market operation which buys and sells its wares to the public. That way, the public can buy them if they want or ignore them. They shouldn't have to buy them simply because the government says they should. The idea that one has to buy something whether one wants it or not is simply a rationalization for exploitation. Taxation is merely robbery under another name. If one doesn't have a choice about what's happening to one's money, then one's simply being robbed.

JE: Do you favor volunteerism when it comes to providing for people who are unable to provide for themselves?

RAW: If we were to make the reforms I've already mentioned, and go full speed ahead with space industrialization and longevity research, then everybody would have space enough, time enough, and eventually intelligence enough to not be in need of charity. Meanwhile, I wouldn't cut welfare for the poor, but I would cut it for the rich.

JE: The criticism is often voiced that ours is a cultureless society, that we have contributed little to the development of western civilization. Do you share this point of view?

RAW: Hell, no! I only need point to the architecture of Frank Lloyd Wright, the design innovations of Buckminster Fuller, and the writings of William Faulkner, Walt Whitman, Ezra Pound, Ernest Hemingway, and Raymond Chandler. I also think jazz has proved to be a singular contribution to the world's music. I think the Modern Jazz Quartet will some day be looked back at in the same way we look back at Vivaldi.

JE: Finally, another object of considerable criticism, although not by you, is television. How do you assess the overall impact of television on modern society?

RAW: Oh, man, there you've got me on one of my favorite subjects. I really think television is 100 times better than most literary intellectuals admit. I think that *Mary Hartman, Mary Hartman* in its two seasons on the air was better than anything done in movies, in novels, or on Broadway at the time. As far as I am concerned, television was the major art medium of the country for those two seasons. Movies, the stage, and literature were totally out-done. The combination of social realism, coupled with black comedy, was masterful. They really made it work! In looking at the show from minute-to-minute, you never knew whether you were going to laugh or cry. The artistic ambiguity was handled brilliantly. I think there has been a lot of other good things on television, too. Since most science fiction fans despise "trekkies," let me go on record as saying that I'm an ardent "trekkie" myself. I love the show. I also think *The Prisoner* is as good as any movie of our generation. In brief, I think television has come in for a lot of very unfair criticism. Of course, it's primarily the fault of the networks themselves. It's extremely irritating to look at something first-rate, only to have it interrupted by those idiotic commercials every seven minutes.

www.ingramcontent.com/pod-product-compliance
Lightning Source LLC
Chambersburg PA
CBHW031333040426
42443CB00005B/316

*9 7 8 1 4 3 4 4 3 4 2 8 9 *